Born Again to Serve with Love

DAILY PRAYER AND MEDITATION BOOK

MICHAEL PETROSINO

Copyright © 2024 by Mike Petrosino

All rights reserved.

Published by Red Penguin Books

Bellerose Village, New York

ISBN

978-1-63777-642-1 / 978-1-63777-643-8

No part of this book may be reproduced in any form or by any electronic or mechanical means, including information storage and retrieval systems, without written permission from the author, except for the use of brief quotations in a book review.

Start your day with Jesus

Preface

The inspired writings from this book have come from my faith in Christ Jesus and the Holy Spirit of Truth! Since my enlightenment (spiritual epiphany) took place in a dark time in my life, while facing a lot of issues, many may doubt the inspiration that the Holy Spirit had on me or these writings; yet, it is very accurate and appropriate to give God all the Glory! Before I started these inspired writings, I had no peace or direction. Now the peace of the Lord has not left me, and I feel born again; a true spiritual rebirth, through faith in Christ Jesus! Most of these writings are inspired, with very little thinking involved. They come all of a sudden and I just write it out, as it comes! Actually trying to express it to the readers now, forms a challenge to me. Trying to explain a spiritual experience, is not an easy task; yet, it is a beautiful experience to go through! I have had the pleasure of sharing these writings all over the world and receiving positive reactions from many people! This book is a compilation of many writings over a 5 year period. The writings in this book consist of many virtues to live by, through faith in Christ Jesus; as well as sharing the love of Christ with the doubters and steadfast believers. Moreover, it is about becoming that which you seek in the world, so you search no more! The spiritual truth is, we never had so much, until we gave it all away! It's the paradoxical reward of giving! Furthermore, my hope in putting this book together, is to reach more people in all kinds of situations and bring light into darkness for those who suffer; as well as make a good day better for many through faith in Christ Jesus!

January 1

As disciples of Christ Jesus, we look to feed the world with the truth of the Messiah! Jesus is He! As we emulate the love of Jesus, our character is transformed from self centered, to God centered! We look to sow peace and not discord! The harmony of our love speaks through our efforts of service for the less fortunate! We feed the world with the love of God, through sharing the good news of Christ Jesus! We share the wisdom of God, by reading His word from Christ Jesus! We feed the world with the provisions that God provides, in Jesus' mighty name; who is the Bread of life! Nothing fills us up, like feeding another with food, wisdom and the love from God; through faith in Christ Jesus and by the power of the Holy Spirit!

January 2

We who know Christ Jesus, rejoice with much enthusiasm! We share the hope in the Lord, with all those who come near! We cannot contain our gratitude, for all that Jesus has done; and all that He is still doing for those who put their hope in Him! We are the church of faith; and our location is our hearts! We sing praises of love, as we help the less fortunate! Blessed are those who have faith in Christ Jesus! In Jesus' mighty name, may we move away from evil, as we sow love into the world!

January 3

The heart of Christ Jesus is love; and no love is greater than the love that laid down His life for His friends! Our walk in faith is to emulate this endless love, through faith in Christ Jesus! The change is radical; and some may reject it, because they aren't ready for it! Become it anyway! For we are called out of darkness and into the light of love! Be the light and reflect Jesus' love, by acts of kindness to all!

January 4

Lord, help us to focus on things above; rather than things below! Help us to stand for virtue and not fall for vice! The temptations of this world are strong when entertained; God help us to not entertain that which is contrary to thy will! In Jesus' mighty name, may we all aspire to be righteous; as God is righteous! May we look past all insults; and carry the peace of the Lord from place to place! May the negativity from people, provoke patience and love from us! May we be examples of a Christian (Christ like) today! In the loving name of Jesus, we pray!

January 5

As we lay down our pride at the foot of the cross and stop looking for admiration from the Lost; we pick up humility from holy surrender to the Lord! What we want out of people and life, takes a back seat to the things we can give and do for those in need! In Jesus' mighty name, may our motives change from self, to thinking of the needs of someone else!

Things to focus on today!

Be the joy (Jesus first, others second and yourself third) in the day! Stay positive and don't let yesterday's issues, become today's problems!

January 6

The Lord wants us on the road that leads to life everlasting! Christ Jesus is that road! No maps are necessary; only the word of God in your heart! Christ Jesus is the word! Faith in Yeshua is an extension of love to all! Faith with works, is service! The greatest among us, is a servant to all! Do not fear the opinions of the lost; only guide them through faith in Christ Jesus! We are all lost without God! No one knows, but God; and Christ Jesus is one with the Father! In Jesus' mighty name, may we stay on the road of truth; and not be detoured by the temptation of lies!

January 7

Where we are feeling strong, let's be there for those that are feeling weak! Let's bring encouraging words, to the discouraged! Let's see where we can serve someone in need today! Let's be the great (LOVE) in this day for all! In the loving name of Jesus/Yeshua, we look to serve and not be served!

Words to remember:
    Believe in Gods creation; He made us competent to overcome all things!

January 8

As we feed those that are hungry for love, we thank the Lord with our deeds! Christ Jesus knows our hearts; and wants that, more than words! As we do for the sick, poor, doubters, imprisoned, hungry and disabled; we do for the Lord! In the mighty name of Jesus, may we look to give with thanksgiving in our hearts, minds and spirits!

Quote for the day:
    It's not about getting and having; it's about giving and helping!

January 9

How far we have come by taking Christ Jesus into our hearts! How far we all need to go! God knows we fall short on so many levels! We fall short in our thoughts and what we think; in our words and what we say; in our deeds and what we do! Yeshua Hamashiach/Jesus the Messiah, has saved us through faith and not by works; so no one can boast! We yearn to be righteous and fall short; yet we still repent in our hearts; as we abide in Christ Jesus! Lord God, help us all to live according to thy word; who is Christ Jesus! In Jesus' mighty name, we pray!

January 10

The message is hope from the truth of Christ Jesus! In that truth is freedom from sin and all lies! Liberty is found in Yeshua/Jesus! We move away from sin and embrace every virtue to serve those in need! We do every good act to bring Glory to God! Peace becomes our shadow, from the principles of love, that Jesus the Christ taught us all!

Things to remember:
 Do not bargain and negotiate with sin or you will become its prey!

January 11

We who look to live by the word of God, through faith in His Son Jesus, who is the word; will be character assassinated by pretentious people, who doubt and believe! Let that negativity motivate you to love more than ever before! Even God in the flesh as Jesus, was put down and judged by the lost! Still He asked the Father to forgive them; for they know not what they do! Look how far we have come! We still have far to go! Enjoy the journey; and don't let any of the haters derail you from your primary purpose of serving all in love; through faith in Christ Jesus! We are all sinners on our best day; and we can move away from sin, through faith in Christ Jesus; and by emulating His love to all those that deserve it; and to those that don't!

January 12

Lord God, we surrender what we think we know; so what is truth, can come into our hearts, minds and spirits to save our souls! Jesus the Christ, is that truth! We who have been lost; and can get lost, from the many temptations in this world; ask for guidance from the Holy Spirit of truth! May we abide in that truth and may that truth abide in us all, through faith in the Son of God; Christ Jesus is He! In Jesus' mighty name, we pray!

January 13

The word of the Lord, is Christ Jesus! As the word becomes more in me, my desire to sin becomes less! As I take Christ Jesus into my heart completely; His love completes me! No darkness of sin is welcome in His light; but He welcomes all sinners to come to Him and repent! I am a sinner who loves the Lord; but if I say I have faith and don't serve others, I am delusional, as I deceive myself! Faith without works is dead; when my belief in God, doesn't line up with serving the Lord! I have been crippled in spirit for a long time; yet through repentance from my sins, working together with my faith in Christ Jesus, my sins have been forgiven! Now I walk in the ways of love and share the good news with all! My motives have changed from self seeking, to serving the less fortunate among us, in Jesus' mighty name!

January 14

We who are inspired by the prophetic message, from the Holy Spirit of Truth, preach the message of hope; through faith in Christ Jesus! May the Holy Spirit give us the words, that open the closed minded, to the truth of Yeshua Hamashiach/Jesus the Messiah! May the rich reward that comes from the inheritance of salvation, through faith in the Son of God; touch the poor in spirit, from the hope we convey to all with love! May all those lost in their sinful ways, find themselves in the truth of Gods word; Christ Jesus is that word! May the repentance of their sins, work in tandem (together), with their faith in Christ Jesus! In Jesus' mighty name, we pray!

January 15

God has no opinion; for He is truth! We who have many opinions, need to follow His truth; through Christ Jesus, who is one with the truth of God! Let's not lean on our own understanding; but on every truth that came from God, through Christ Jesus! The word became flesh; to guide us to the spirit, through repentance and faith in the Son of God! Christ Jesus is He! To live by the word of God, is to stand for the truth of Christ Jesus and resist the lie of the world! In Jesus' mighty name!

January 16

As we become a new creation through faith in Christ Jesus; we are sanctified (set apart as Holy) by the power of the Holy Spirit! Now the Lord is alive in us by that power! We must not desecrate (treat something holy with violent disrespect) ourselves any longer! For as Christ Jesus is Holy, we must remain holy! This is our new aspiration (a hope or ambition of achieving something) through faith in Christ Jesus! We speak to the doubters in character first; and words second! We do everything in our power to take the high road (to behave in a moral way, when others are behaving immorally) as we serve all with love! In Jesus' most Holy name, we aspire to emulate Yeshua/Jesus in everything that we do!

January 17

May we as disciples of Christ Jesus, feed all those who are hungry! Moreover, may we share our faith in the Son of God, with all those who are poor in spirit! For those who are lonely, may we comfort them with friendship! For all those lost in their sorrow, may we share the word of God as a compass; to guide them to Christ Jesus! For all those who endured abuse and have been mistreated, may we as Christians comfort them with unconditional love! In Jesus' mighty name, may we do all things, as we would want done to us!

January 18

The Lord is ready to guide the willing; so be willing! The Lord is the way to peace; so embrace the Lord with all your heart! The love of the Lord brings light into darkness; so stay in the light and do what is right! Christ Jesus is the Lord! Know the truth of God and know peace! Christ Jesus is the Prince of Peace! Emulate His love; and peace will not elude you, but become your shadow from His great light! Once we internalize the truth of Yeshua/Jesus, the new creation has come into fruition; in Christ Jesus' mighty name!

January 19

As we come to know the Lord deeper in our faith, our yearning to share the good news (Gospel) becomes greater! It stands against the lies and false belief systems of this lost generation! It stands up with a steadfast (unwavering) faith against the negative opinions about the Son of God; Christ Jesus is He! The truth of Yeshua/Jesus is the only light in us all! We share that light with love; because He is the love that laid down His life for the forgiveness of sins! In Jesus' mighty name, may we who believe in the Son of Man, share that truth with all those who are willing to receive it!

January 20

I seek the Lord with all my heart, yet I lack much! I open my mind to the word of God, but understand little! I analyze what I do and don't do, but I don't change much! I utilize the truth of Christ Jesus to serve others, but I can do more! Search me oh Lord; where I fall Short, help me to change, so that I may be in compliance with thy will! In Jesus' mighty name, I pray!

It's amazing; God is everywhere through faith in Christ Jesus and His love brings us such peace to share with the world!

January 21

God is; and what He wills, will be, as it is to be! He is Lord of Lords, and King of Kings! One Spirit with His only begotten Son Jesus/Yeshua! We surrender all that we are and all that we aren't at the foot of the cross! Bless us with your truth and may we who know it, by the power of the Holy Spirit; never turn away from it! Protect us from the temptations of this lost generation! Help us in the mighty name of Jesus, to guide the willing, to your word! In thy most Holy name, we pray!

January 22

How we weep without you Lord! May we, who have moved away in thought, talk or our walk, turn back to you with contrite spirits (showing sincere remorse)! In Christ Jesus' mighty name, may we stand for the truth of the Gospel; and not fall for the wage of sin! May we not entertain that which is contrary to thy will! Help us Lord, to stay beyond reproach (disapproval); so that we may guide those lost in sin to you! In Jesus' Holy name, we pray!

January 23

As we take off the filthy rags of sin and are cleansed through being baptized by the Holy Spirit of truth, through faith in Christ Jesus; we put on the Garment of righteousness, through our intercessor Yeshua/Jesus! We share the good news (Gospel) with excitement! There is hope in the Lord Jesus; take Him into your heart and change your sinful ways; into virtues that serve all! For we are Representatives of Christ Jesus! In Jesus' mighty name, may we emulate the Holiness of the Lord!

January 24

As we stop competing with each other and start supporting one another; the humility of the Lord becomes our shadow, from His great light! Peace comes into fruition, by putting others and their needs before our own! When we stop looking to the world for what we can get; and start looking for what we can give; then peace becomes our mindset, from the generosity of love! When we change the way we approach people and look at things with the projection of Christ Jesus' love, everything changes for the better in our minds, spirits and relationships! In Jesus' mighty name, help us God, to emulate thy Son; who is the Prince of Peace!

January 25

For us who believe in Christ Jesus, there's a burning desire to share the Holy Gospel with everyone, so they don't burn in hell! Repent now and put your faith in Jesus, the Christ! Thank you Lord, for your Holy Sacrifice! Jesus wouldn't have gone through the horrific death on the cross, filled with Excruciating pain, if He wasn't trying to save us, from the everlasting pain of Hell! This gift is embraced with faith in the Son of God; Christ Jesus is He! We move away from every sinful lie in this world: and move towards the truth of Christ Jesus! This is the very essence of repentance! We must lead by example, by abiding (to conform to) to the truth of Christ Jesus! In doing so, we will not be hypocritical, as blind guides are!

January 26

I am a human being, born again (spiritual rebirth) to serve all in love! It's only through faith in Christ Jesus and the emulation (effort to match) of His amazing Grace, that I project authentic (genuine) love to anyone! I can only aspire to emulate this love; its only through Yeshua/Jesus and His intercession, that my love is perfected to all! May the attraction of loving kindness, be the promotion (providing active encouragement) of the Holy Gospel we share with the world! As we repent from our sins and put on the garment of virtue, our character speaks louder than words! In Christ Jesus' Holy name, may we all serve one another, as Yeshua served all of us!

January 27

There are many things that can lure us away from the truth of God, if we don't stay anchored in the truth of Christ Jesus! All that is good is in Christ; and no dark sin is welcomed in His light! He welcomes every sinner into His loving light of mercy! In that Grace is repentance; and in that faith, is freedom from being a slave to sin! We embrace this Grace, and know the freedom from thy truth Lord! In Jesus' mighty name, help us all to spread the good news of the Gospel!

January 28

I am content in all situations, because Christ Jesus is my strength in weakness and my hope! I stay grateful for all that God has blessed me with; and I don't complain about the stuff I don't have! I count all my blessings and none of my woes; I count you all as friends; and none as foes! There's no envy or jealousy in me today; because I'm not trying to bring glory to my name; therefore, I am content! All Glory belongs to God the Father, who I serve, through faith in thy Son Jesus!

January 29

All things I do in the name of Jesus/Yeshua! It's amazing how much we get out of life, when we give it all away! We never had so much love, until we gave someone all of ours! We become the peace we seek and search no more, when we emulate the Lords love; now the peace of the Lord doesn't elude us, but becomes our shadow, from the Lords great light! We become the principles of peace, love, friendship and many other virtues; now happiness has become our attitude, by returning the kindness with gratitude!

January 30

When we persevere through the trials in this life, we will build the character that speaks louder than words! It is faith that gives strength to the weak! Our faith is in Christ Jesus; and our truth comes from His words! The word that is alive in us, is Christ Jesus; Holy in Spirit and in Truth! We sing with elated spirits, that have found hope, in the Son of God! Furthermore, we emulate His love to all those that are poor in spirit and lack in faith! We invite those that doubt, with love and authentic kindness! In Jesus' mighty name, may we duplicate the love of Christ Jesus; to all those lonely and faithless!

January 31

There are those in the world that will deny the truth of Christ Jesus! Their hearts are cold and their minds are closed! As for us who believe in the Son of God, you are our light in darkness and our hope in despair! You are our joy in difficult times and the truth to every lie in this world! Jesus is the Christ; and we stand for this truth, without participating in contentious arguments with the atheist or agnostic! For He is the Prince of Peace; and we extend that peace, even to the doubter! The Holy Spirit is alive in God's faithful children! In Jesus' mighty name, may we all stand together in the faith of Yeshua/Jesus; and not deny His truth to anyone who doubts!

February 1

Thank you Lord Jesus for your instructions on how to live! May I be compliant and not defiant! May I not be obtuse (slow to understand) to repentance; but quick to listen to your reproof (disapproval) and change my ways! For you are my God and your ways are now my ways! May my faith in thy Son please thee! Thank you God for your loving mercy and Grace, through faith in thy Son Jesus! In Jesus' mighty name, may I stay beyond reproach (such that no criticism can be made/blameless)!

February 2

As your word is Holy, I am to remain Holy! As it is, I have been unholy and repent through faith in thy Son! As the old has passed away, may my sins be forgotten through faith! Heavenly Father God, your love is expressed in the righteousness of thy Son Jesus! I hunger for righteousness, as I die to all selfishness! Help me to be obedient to thy will, in all that I do! In Jesus' mighty name, may I put others before myself; in thy Holy name, I pray!

February 3

The sin in this life is tempting to the one who bargains and negotiates with it; as one who entertains its pleasures, and decides to look away from the torment that follows! We ask God for help in these weak moments, through faith in Christ Jesus; who has defeated all sin! God knows our struggles and that's why He came down from Heaven, in the Spirit of His Son! Who died for us all; to save us from the wage of sin (death)! Those who know Christ Jesus, can't rest in sin; but have a contrite spirit (remorseful and repenting) that looks to honor the great gift of salvation through faith in Yeshua/Jesus! In Jesus' mighty name, we pray!

February 4

As we internalize your word God, through Faith in Christ Jesus and by the power of the Holy Spirit; the word of God becomes alive in us! God, You have entered our hearts, through faith in your precious Son! May the good works that you started, be completed, in Jesus' mighty name! If anything in us, stands in the way of your will, and to guide others, we ask that you remove it! May the patient love of Christ Jesus, rest upon us all; to serve others and not ourselves! In Jesus' mighty name, we pray!

February 5

Heavenly Father,

    We honor you with Faith in your Son Jesus/Yeshua! For you and the Son are one Love and one Light! Whoever believes in thee, shall never walk in darkness! You make our paths straight with your Holy Righteousness! As we abide (conform to) in you, you abide in us! You are the only true Father and we are your children! In Jesus' mighty name, may we all be willing to change our sinful behavior; and may that willingness be acceptable to you, through faith in Christ Jesus! For you are our God and Father; and we have reverence (deep respect) for you Lord!

February 6

I come to you Lord, with every thought that is sinful and ask that you forgive me for what I have thought of, continue to think and what I have failed to think! Please guide my thoughts Christ Jesus! I come to you Lord, with every word I have spoken that is sinful and ask for forgiveness! Forgive me for what I have said, continue to say and what I have failed to say! Guide every word from my mouth by the Holy Spirit of truth, through faith in Christ Jesus! Lord God, forgive me for every sinful act I committed, still commit and for the way I fail to act! Guide me to live by virtue and not by vice; for I have a contrite spirit and I repent in Jesus' mighty name!

February 7

We come to you, Jesus, with every temptation and surrender it at the foot of the cross! We come as sinners; and through faith in Yeshua, we leave with hope in salvation! Lord God, you take us off the road to destruction; and put us on the road to righteousness! It's only through thy word and faith in thee, that we navigate through many temptations in life! On our own accord, we fall short of thy Glory! All Glory be to thy Spirit, in Christ Jesus! In Jesus' mighty name, we submit all sinful temptations to thee!

February 8

As we journey through each day, may we surrender all things, in every way! In Yeshua's mighty name, may every thought that is not Holy, be cast down and replaced by virtue! May every word spoken, be in compliance with love and truth! May each step taken, be to serve and not be served! May our goals be to emulate Christ Jesus, in every way; everyday! In Jesus' Holy name, we pray!

Find peace in this!
    The validation of Gods love, is seen in the Holy Sacrifice of Christ Jesus! In that, we find refuge for our souls!

February 9

My God, who has rescued me from the eternal flames of Torment; through faith in thy Son, who is of thy Spirit of Truth! I love thee with all my heart, soul, mind and strength! Guide me in thy ways and help me to not stray from thy path! In Jesus' mighty name, I pray!

Practice being the change you seek in the world!

Be the positivity you seek in the world and search no more; then a positive attitude (kindness, friendly, optimistic, generous and much more) won't elude you, but become your shadow, from the Lords great light!

February 10

Your word God, guides your faithful servants by the Holy Spirit of truth; through faith in Christ Jesus! You help us in our journeys, to not be mislead by the temptations of this world! We praise your name in our difficulties and sufferings; because we put all our hope in you and the life to come! We look past the insults and bring your love to those who are lost and confused! We are steadfast in our faith in Christ Jesus; and we look to emulate His love in all that we do! We do all things to bring Glory to our Father, who Art in Heaven; in Jesus' mighty name!

February 11

I'm thankful for the Holy sacrifice of Christ Jesus, for the forgiveness of sins; for I am a sinner! I'm thankful for the Holy Spirit of truth alive in me, so I can be every good thing I seek, through emulating the love of Christ Jesus to the least among us; and putting them before myself in true humility! My list of gratitude never ends with all the things I can see, hear, touch, taste, smell and think! Furthermore, all the places I can go and do for others with authentic love! All the people in my life and the toxic people I can love and help, as well as walk away from! To know much more than ever before and to know, I know little! I'm grateful for Christ Jesus being my strength in weakness and knowing I'm weak! I know a new freedom and happiness from my faith in Christ Jesus; and from being the change I seek, from the transformation of accountability! I've changed many defects of character, from taking responsibility for the chaos I caused and turned them into productive virtues, that are always good and never bad! To know I'm never good, but aspire to be every second of every day! All Glory to God, through faith in Christ Jesus!

February 12

May our ambitions be to feed the poor in spirit, with the word of God; Jesus the Christ, is that word! May we hunger for your truth, like a disciple breaking a fast; Jesus the Christ, is that truth! Heavenly Father, may we aspire to live according to your commandments and be saved by our faith in Christ Jesus! In Jesus' mighty name, we pray!

Words to meditate on;
Be the peace (compassionate, loving, flexible, objective, peaceful restraint and much more) you seek from emulating Christ Jesus' love and search no more; then peace will not elude you, but become your shadow from the Lords great light!

February 13

When I completely surrender myself to God through Christ Jesus, I am no longer trying to enforce my will upon others; I am however, becoming transformed by the will of God! My focus becomes about what I can do for others and not self! I never had so much love, until I gave you all of mine! Furthermore, nothing fills me up, like feeding you with food, friendship, compassion and the wisdom of God, through faith in Christ Jesus! May we all become more like Jesus and less like ourselves, through Holy surrender, in Jesus' mighty name!

February 14

As I inhale the truth of Christ Jesus, I expel the lie in me that lead me astray from you! Lord God, you have shown me great mercy through faith in your Son Jesus! Now that I know the truth of Christ Jesus, help me emulate His ways in my journey! May I stand for your truth, in all that I do! To know the truth of Christ Jesus and live contrary to it, causes unbearable torment! Heavenly Father, I pray that you strengthen anyone who is struggling with sin! Set them free from the torment of sin and may they adopt the righteousness of your Son, so they know peace beyond all understanding; in the mighty name of Jesus!

February 15

We thank you Lord for your Holy Sacrifice! We repent in Jesus' mighty name, from all iniquity! May the Holy Spirit guide us in truth; so we don't entertain the lie! We are your new creation God; through faith in Christ Jesus! Being new in spirit (sanctified), we walk away from the old behavior's that are contrary to thy will! We stay in thy light, with thy love! All that is evil repulses us! We know the torment of sin and we choose the righteous path! We walk this path with Christ Jesus; who intercedes on our behalf! On our own, we fall short in many ways; but we aspire to live by virtue! In Jesus' mighty name!

February 16

The Lord is Jesus; the Son of the living God! He is the Light of the World, who saves us all from darkness! Put your trust in Him and know peace! Lean not on your own understanding; but on every word that comes from God! Be not dismayed by the world's destructiveness; but know peace from Gods promise, through Christ Jesus! Have faith in the Messiah; Jesus is He! Turn away from all that is evil and stand for the love that comes from God! Jesus is that love! The forgiveness of God is a gift from faith! Take the leap and know everlasting peace! In Jesus' mighty name, may we all know the everlasting peace, through faith in Christ Jesus!

February 17

We are the ripple effect of Gods love, through faith in Christ Jesus! The generous love of God, gives us plenty to reach all those poor in spirit! Christ Jesus gives us much hope to give to those who feel overwhelmed by the negative projections of their mind! The Holy Spirit guide's us in truth; to guide those lost in the lie of this world! In Jesus' mighty name, may we as disciples of Christ, guide the lost to the Son of God!

Meditate on the principles of love:
    Be the principles of love that are virtuous! Remember, that we never had so much love, until we gave all of ours!

February 18

As I travel closer to the truth, I see how lost I was in the lie! My honesty is contingent on revealing the lie I denied for so long! The truth of God has brought light into the darkness in my life! Many belief systems I defended and protected, turned out to be erroneous to the truth of Christ Jesus! Now that I can see where I've been blind, the changes to be in compliance with the will of God can happen! I must surrender all, so I can begin to receive! May the truth of Christ Jesus set us free, from the lies in the world and the lies in me! In Jesus' mighty name, I pray!

February 19

To bring peace to others is my daily goal! To speak kind words in a gentle way, is to convey love! To allow others to proceed before me, is an act of kindness, that is appreciated often! As I become the peace I seek, I search no more! I share that which I become to all! The more I share the peace I have, the deeper my peace becomes! May we all emulate the Prince of Peace; who is Christ Jesus!

Things to remember;
   We surrender the opinions of others, because they are not the truth of God! Moreover, we surrender the opinion of our self; for we are not the truth of God either! We don't allow our inner critic to dictate how we see ourselves! We rest in the unconditional love of Christ Jesus and know peace!

February 20

In serving the Lord, let's walk in the light! Don't let the enticing flesh take root in your mind! Meditate on the word of God, through faith in Christ Jesus and you will not entertain sin! If we go after the lie in the world, torment becomes our shadow! If we seek peace, through faith in Christ Jesus, freedom from sin becomes our goal! We must plow through the many temptations in this life, with the Holy Spirit of Truth! We are not alone! Christ Jesus is always with us! What we can't do alone, we can accomplish through faith in Christ Jesus! In Jesus' mighty name, we ask for help with the many temptations that try to lure us into sin!

February 21

As a disciple of Christ Jesus and by the power of the Holy Spirit of Truth, I serve the Lord with true humility! Today, may I put all Gods children before myself! May I guide others with the true message of the Gospel and not dilute the truth for anyone! May I do all things in love; and emulate the love of the Lord to all! In Jesus' mighty name, I pray!

Faith in Christ Jesus is more than believing, it is trusting in the Lord completely, with a steadfast (unwavering) faith!

February 22

How can we be gentle around a coarse (rough, rude, crude and vulgar) heart? We do this through faith in the Prince of Peace; Christ Jesus is He! When we emulate the love of Christ Jesus, we don't delight in evil! We rejoice in all that is truth; which is good in the Lord! We share instead of take! We introduce lawlessness to the love of Christ Jesus from our steadfast faith, being projected in character towards those lost in debauchery! We educate the lost by the word of God; through faith in Christ Jesus! It's a two way street called Willingness Ave, in the city of Hope! In Jesus' mighty name, we ask for help in every situation that avails itself, as an opportunity to save a soul!

February 23

As the wisdom of the Lord rests upon us, may we stay beyond reproach! For the doubter is watching and the opportunity to guide to Christ Jesus lies within our character! We have been called out of darkness and into the light with Christ Jesus! In that light is love and every good virtue that precedes it! In Jesus' mighty name, may we all walk in the light of Christ Jesus and guide the lost by our example!

Internalize this:
 Be the love you seek and anger will be a lost foe! Be transformed by the word of God and know peace! In Gods love is the peace beyond all understanding!

February 24

How we hunger for the word, now that the word of God is alive in us! Christ Jesus is the word; and our faith in Christ Jesus, is the bread that feeds that hunger! The bread that came down from Heaven, is shared in all nations and among all those starving for salvation! They will not be disappointed! May they digest the message of hope, from the loving sacrifice, for the forgiveness of sins! In Jesus' mighty name, let's all share the word; with those that are hungry for it and poor in spirit!

February 25

Stay in the yoke with Christ Jesus and know the peace that comes from the Lord! You are not alone in your loss, trials or tribulations! For where you are weak, Christ Jesus is strong! Lean not on your own understanding, but on every word that proceedeth out of the mouth of God; through faith in Christ Jesus! Look to serve and not be served; and know peace! Look to understand, than to be understood; and become the peace you seek! Be the principles of peace through Christ Jesus' light of love and no darkness can overtake you! In Jesus' mighty name, help us all to stay in the yoke, with the Son of God!

February 26

No one's opinion is the truth of Christ Jesus! Therefore, we must not allow other people's opinions to dictate how we feel about ourselves! Moreover, we should not allow our inner critic to dictate how we feel about ourselves; because we aren't the truth of God either! We should step out of our feelings often and look at ourselves objectively! When we do this, we can see clearly if the feelings are even accurate with the circumstances! More often than not, they aren't! It must be noted, that all this self reflection, can make us extremely self centered! We pray in Jesus' mighty name, that we avoid that!

February 27

All things must come to an end! As in the end of ones life; who by faith, took Christ Jesus into their heart and lived to serve others with love; always giving Glory to God! They must say goodbye to this sluggish body of pain and all earthly things, as they move to the kingdom of Heaven; in a vibrant spirit of light, with no pain and the fullness of our Creator's love! Oh how we yearn to be with you Lord!

Keep the faith:
Lord God, you are the light over darkness, the love over hate, the righteousness over sin, the victory over defeat! In Jesus' mighty name, you are our life over death!

February 28

As I surrender myself to the Lord, I ask Christ Jesus to remove from me anything that is not in compliance with His will! I have a contrite spirit (The desire for atonement; a contrite sinner; repenting) and fall short of Gods Glory! Dearest Jesus, please intercede on my behalf and help me to stay yoked to you! I love you with all my heart, spirit, mind and strength! In Jesus' mighty name, I pray!

Surrendering all hidden motives, is our goal for peace:
    May the word of God, through Christ Jesus be alive in me; as I die to self daily!

Leap Year Writing: February 29

God help me to search my mind and surrender all that is not in compliance with your will! By the power of the Holy Spirit, through Christ Jesus your Son, reveal in me all darkness and remove it with your loving light! May I forgive all in the world, like you have forgiven all of me through Faith in your Son Jesus! Thank you for freeing me from the bondage of sin! May I be a slave to your righteousness through sanctification! May my life be a power of example of your great mercy and sovereign power! All Glory to you God, through your mighty Son Jesus!

March 1

We need to be kind and meek to all! We need to be humble with faith in Christ Jesus! We need to be lead by the word of God; furthermore, we need to always keep it sacred in our hearts, minds, and spirits! We must be trusting children of God, that don't get distracted by the things in this world; that take away the authenticity of our relationship with the FATHER! Our vulnerability in Faith, must be as steadfast as children of the most High God, through Christ Jesus! We must allow God's love to be our universal language to all believers in Jesus and an etiquette to all future Christian's!

March 2

Do not delight in malice, so that others might understand your pain; But be transformed by the power of the Holy Spirit, through Faith in Christ Jesus! May His truth set you free from your folly and may His righteousness become your shadow! See people with negative attitudes, as an opportunity to be benevolent! May the darkness in this world, propel you to bring the light of the Lord, into every situation! In Christ Jesus' mighty name, we pray!

March 3

As we put all of our trust in the Lord, we free ourselves from fear! The deeper our trust, the more tranquil our inner peace becomes! Therefore, our peace is contingent on our faith in Christ Jesus and not in self! The journey is an inner one, that is felt and not seen! As is the fruit of faith, that produces peace beyond all understanding! May the peace of Christ Jesus, rest upon you all, like a ray of sunshine after the storm! In the mighty name of Jesus, we pray!

March 4

The love of the Lord sets me free, from the hate in the world and the negativity in me! For where there is love, all good dwells! As I meditate on the love of Christ Jesus, I become one with love! I replace darkness with light and refuse to go back to my sinful ways! I rejoice in the serene freedom of love, that keeps me yoked to the most High God, through our Lord Jesus, the Christ! May our character convey the expression of love to all! To be one with love, is to be one with God!

March 5

Heavenly Father, I come to you and ask that you guide me today; with the Holy Spirit that comes upon me, through Faith in your Son Jesus! Help me to see the part I play, in any chaos in my life or the lives of others! Help me to not force my will upon anybody; but in all my ways to emulate the love of Jesus and be a servant to all! May I serve all your children with love, peace, generosity and humility! May I convey the message of hope about the Grace of God, through faith in Christ Jesus! In the mighty name of Jesus, I ask for your help, to do your will!

March 6

Heavenly Father God, with deep reverence I come to thee, through faith in your Holy Son Jesus! I surrender all of me to you, with the most grateful heart to know you and be in your presence! Your love God, propels me to serve you and all my brothers and sisters! Now that you have revealed your light upon my darkness, I can see through your wonderful Grace, the filthy sins that you have washed away by your Holy Sacrifice! In honoring this great gift from thee, I repent from my sins, like a hand from a hot flame! I only see, because you allow me to see! In now seeing, I guide others to you, so that they may know your love and not your wrath! May your truth be revealed to all, in Jesus' mighty name!

March 7

As I feed on the bread of life, which is Christ Jesus; the truth lives in me and no sin of lies can reside! As I drink the blood of Jesus, which was shed for all; I become one with God through the Son and Sacrifice myself for others in an altruistic (selfless) way! I no longer belong to the world; I now belong to the Father through faith in His Son! Now I can be in the House of the Lord forever, which we call Heaven!

The truth of God is Christ Jesus! That truth defies all logic! God makes the impossible happen! All Glory to God the Father, His Son Jesus and the Holy Spirit!

March 8

All Glory to God the Father, through faith in Christ Jesus! In all humility, may I look to bring Glory to His name and not my own! For you God, are the Creator and I am the creation; anything good that comes from me, comes from you who created it; therefore, I cannot boast! May I embrace your Grace through your Son Jesus and emulate His love to all! May I look to serve and not be served, by showing gratitude in my attitude; as I return your kindness to all!

May the word of God, through Christ Jesus, be alive in me; as I die to self daily!

March 9

The love of Christ Jesus will help us to persevere through anything this world challenges us with! We can do all things through Christ! Fear not! The faithful in Christ Jesus will not be dismayed! May our faith in Christ Jesus be authentically contagious to the doubters in this world! May we be willing to stand alone in faith, than with many lost in doubt and obtuse (slow to understand) to the truth of Christ Jesus! In the mighty name of Jesus, we pray!

Faith in Christ Jesus makes fear dissipate!

March 10

It is only by faith in Christ Jesus that we can please God! For the Father and the Son are one Spirit! As we embrace the truth in faith, all things become possible! Christ Jesus is Truth! His crucifixion and Resurrection from death did happen! He is the only way to the Father! There is no lie that ever came out of His mouth! If anyone doubts Christ Jesus, they are not in good standings with God our Father; nor will they enter the Kingdom of Light! It's not too late to stop defending your erroneous belief system! Be open to receive the Lord and you will receive life forever with God our Father! In Jesus' mighty name, I pray for all doubters!

March 11

When we trust the Lord with all our heart, soul and mind, peace becomes our shadow from the Lords Great Light! Putting all our trust in God, will never disappoint any of us! There is comfort in knowing Christ Jesus! As we understand you more, we become less; and we follow the light that brings peace out of chaos! God you are the most compassionate! Your love takes away all suffering! Our refuge is in you and you alone; through faith in your Son Jesus! As we abide in you, our folly dissipates! How we yearn for your righteousness; as your word guides us correctly! All Glory to you God; and not ourselves! For anything good that comes from us, was created by you!

March 12

The more faith I have in God through Christ Jesus, the less I need from the world or the people in it! As I look to succeed to feed the poor, I stop feeding my greed for more! The more I love God, the less love I need from the world or the people in it! Therefore, I never had so much love, until I gave you all of mine! Nothing fills me up like feeding you with food, love and wisdom that comes from Christ Jesus! As I look to God for everything, the less I need of anything! Furthermore, all that I have with God, I look to share it with everyone! Since He freely gave it to me, so shall I freely give it to you!

March 13

There is no greater accomplishment in this world, than taking Jesus the Christ into your heart; repenting from your sins; and bringing the Holy Gospel to the atheist and agnostic! True freedom follows this journey! Jesus is the truth, that sets us free, from the lies in us, and in the world!

Don't be afraid to share the greatest sacrifice and love that Yeshua/Jesus gave to us! In Jesus' mighty name, may God give us the fortitude, to share the good news about Christ Jesus to the world! May our character and words emulate His authentic love!

March 14

To know Jesus, is to know hope! To believe in Jesus, will keep you free from fear! To abide in Jesus, is to live in truth! To find refuge in Jesus, is to be kept safe from insidious foes! To love Jesus, is to never hate again! To have faith in Jesus, is to live forever in paradise! All good things are found in Christ Jesus!

Without Christ Jesus, man is without God! Know Christ Jesus, and know God; no Jesus, no God! Take the Good Lord into your heart today and make Him your Lord and Savior! Salvation is found only in the Son of God! Yeshua/Jesus is He!

March 15

The closest we can get to God's perfection, is to love authentically with no hidden motives! When we do that, we become one with God and emulate His great light of love; that is beyond words or any understanding! We then become the love we seek in this world and search no more! As a result of this transformation that comes from knowing Christ Jesus, we become more understanding, patient, altruistic and peaceful human beings! In Christ Jesus' mighty name, may the love of Christ Jesus bring light to all darkness!

March 16

We must see the struggle as an opportunity to grow in character, by persevering with faith in the most High God! We get our strength in the struggle, by being in the yoke with Jesus! For where we are weak, He is strong! Moreover, we don't lean on our own understanding, but every word of God! Greater is He that is in me, than he that is in the world! We must not form an opinion of what we think we can endure, but form one from the perspective that God created us to be overcomers through Christ Jesus; and we are blessed beyond any trial, tribulation or tragedy! With God, all things are possible for those who have faith! As our faith in Christ Jesus increases, our problems decrease by the way we look at them, with hope in the Lord!

March 17

I rejoice in the Lord with great Jubilation! For the Grace of God is upon me, through Faith in Christ Jesus! Of myself I fall short of the Glory of God! I am so grateful to know the truth about Jesus, that I want all to know through me; by expressing God's love to all! May my character speak in a generous way, by being kind and humble in spirit to all! May many be intrigued by the acts of compassion that guide the lost to the truth of Christ Jesus; where the light of love envelopes us all! May all chaos that comes from sin dissipate as we embrace the Grace of God; through Faith in His Son, Jesus the Christ!

March 18

We are the church of faith in Christ Jesus! We are not a location that's made of brick, wood or anything else! We carry the message of Hope (Gospel)! We stay steadfast in the truth of Christ Jesus! We stay focused in the word of God! Christ Jesus is the word! We stay calm by meditating on the word! The peace of the Lord becomes our shadow, from Jesus' loving light! When we connect in faith with one another, Christ Jesus is there! It's the faith in Christ Jesus that makes a church special; not the brick or wood! We are the church of faith, that's made of flesh! We stand in spirit and die to self daily! All we seek is to serve the Lord with love, in all that we do! We bring that loving faith from place to place, in Jesus' mighty name, and we call it the CHURCH!

March 19

As children of God through faith in Christ Jesus, we boast about our weaknesses to the world; for where we are weak, Christ Jesus' strength is perfected! Those that feel powerless in this life, can find a new hope in the Lord! As Disciples of Christ, we know the strength found in the love of God; Christ Jesus is that love! We spread the love first and the word second! For what is the word without love? For they work in tandem for God's good purpose, through Christ Jesus! In Jesus' loving name, may we all emulate the love of the Lord, through the word of God!

March 20

I must conform to God's way, through faith in Christ Jesus! If I am obtuse (slow to understand), the torment of sin will motivate me, when the pain gets greater than the reward, from all forms of debauchery (excessive indulgence in sensual pleasures). Once you embrace the truth of Christ Jesus, you want to guide others to His truth! The lie of the world comes in many forms, but the truth only in one form, named Yeshua/Jesus! May we stop fighting the truth of God and embrace the love and peace that is beyond all understanding! May the light of Jesus, eliminate all darkness in our lives!

March 21

We are the church of Christ; through faith in the Son of God! We are the vessels of love, through the extension of kindness to all! We bring to life, the commandment of loving one another, by feeding the hungry! As we serve one another in love, as Christ Jesus has served us; no sin can be found! For in virtue, the light of God is found; through faith in Christ Jesus! We are the Church of Faith! In this faith we can do every good thing, through Christ Jesus!

March 22

My heart leaps with great joy, for the love given by Christ Jesus! My mind finds comfort in the hope of Grace, through Faith in the Son of God! Our sinful ways have been washed away by his loving sacrifice! Our Lord has defeated the wage of sin, which brings death! He has risen! May the Holy Spirit be upon me, to emulate the love of God, through Christ Jesus and share the good news (Gospel) with all!

When you are the love you seek through faith in Christ Jesus, love is everywhere you look!

March 23

In Jesus' Holy name, may we be a friend and not a foe! May we look to serve and not be served! May we see people's lack of understanding, as an opportunity to project authentic love and educate them with kindness! May we see the one's that are suffering, as an opportunity to show compassion and listen with empathy! May we be awake to participate in social relationships with all; Bringing the truth of Christ Jesus, as the way for the day that never ends!

March 24

Many caught in their folly (lacking good sense) have perished! By their malice (desire to do evil), they provoked the hand of God! May the Lord save us from the wage of sin! May the Holy Spirit of truth, help us all to speak the truth about salvation to the lost! May we stay sanctified (set apart as holy) in the spirit, mind and body; as well as die to self daily! May Christ Jesus be our strength, where we are weak! May Jesus bless all who have faith in Him and help us guide the doubters! In Jesus' mighty name, we pray!

March 25

Through faith in Christ Jesus, we have a promise to be reconciled with God! My Hope is in this promise and the gift is immediate peace, through the Holy Spirit of truth! I ask God the father, through his Son and in union with the Holy Spirit of truth, to guide me, to guide others, to the truth of Jesus and the hope that brings peace beyond all understanding! May the hope in the Lord eliminate all anxiety! May the faith in Christ Jesus conquer all your fears!

March 26

Dearest Father God, we thank you for the most precious gift you could ever give! You have given your lost children a way back to you; through the Holy Sacrifice of your innocent Son Jesus! The innocence of Christ Jesus, took the wage of sin from the guilty upon Himself; so we could be one family with the Father, through Faith in Him! May we share this awesome gift of love with all, in Christ Jesus' mighty name!

To be content with little or much, comes from our hope in the Lord!

March 27

As we put on the yoke to be one with Christ Jesus, we abide in His love, that is one with God! This makes the difficulties in this life easier and we carry less! We don't allow the world to dictate our attitude; for our trust in the Lord conquers all negativity! We are filled with love that doesn't run out and we share this abundance with all! May the peace that comes from the love of God be upon us all, in the mighty name of Jesus/Yeshua!

"Let's Remember"
    The beginning of want, is the end of gratitude!

March 28

Heavenly Father,

Through your Son Jesus, I surrender all of me, to be in compliance with thee! May my folly (lack of good sense; foolishness) be turned into wisdom, to guide the lost to you! May my vice (immoral or wicked behavior), be turned into righteousness, so that I remain Holy with thee; who has cleansed my sin! May your love, overcome all malice (the intention or desire to do evil) in me; so that kindness and peace is brought to all! In the mighty name of Jesus, may I project your light everywhere I go!

March 29

Heavenly Father, we come to you through your Son Jesus, who sets us free from all iniquity! We put your hedge of protection on, through faith in your Son! Moreover, we focus on bringing the peace from the Lord, into every situation! Your word helps us stay in the truth of Jesus and not to be mislead, by the enticing lie of the world (sin)! We embrace the truth of God through Christ Jesus; and allow that truth to set us free in every way! May God's hedge of protection, be upon all who yearn for the truth and love that comes from knowing Christ Jesus!

March 30

As I express the love of Christ Jesus, I bring the light of the Lord into the darkness of sin! I guide the tormented sufferer out with the promise of Grace, through faith in Christ Jesus; for with that faith, is freedom from sin and torment! As I embrace the truth of Christ Jesus, I no longer bargain or negotiate with the lie of sin in any way! I want nothing to interfere with the relationship I have with the Prince of Peace! May we become the peace of the Lord, by expressing the love of God to all; In the mighty name of Jesus, we pray!

March 31

Now that we know Christ Jesus as our Savior from the wage (death) of sin; may we put an end to every desire of debauchery that is not in compliance with the will of God! May our intimate relationship with Jesus, suffice (be enough) in the fulfillment of love! As we become one with the Father, through faith in His Son Jesus; no sin is welcomed! With great joy we live by virtue to serve the Lord and not by the desires of our flesh!

May the word of God, through Christ Jesus, be alive in me, as I die to self daily!

April 1

Jesus is the breath of life for all eternity! May we put all of our hope in Him and trust that it will produce ever lasting peace and love! Nothing in this world is more important than our faith in Christ Jesus! We were created for God's Glory and not our own! Embrace the truth of Jesus and stop listening to the lies of the doubter! May you accept the truth of Christ Jesus and allow that truth to set you free!

Without Christ Jesus, man is without God! Know Christ Jesus, and know God; no Christ Jesus, no God! It's really that simple! If you have doubts, do your research before you make the biggest decision of your life! Without the Son of God, it's all for naught (nothing)!

April 2

Some will say I know the Lord, but continue to live by sin! others will turn from sin (Repent) as best they can, and ask the Lord for help where they are weak! To know the Lord of light, is to stay in the light by faith; and dying to self daily! May Jesus the Son of light, that is one with the FATHER of light, bless all who are lost in darkness and desire His righteousness! May we as followers of Christ Jesus, set an example of righteousness and love to all non-believers! In Jesus' mighty name!

The Lamb Of God

You took our sins, on the cross; so all would be forgiven; and not one lost! You taught us forgiveness, through faith in You; because Grace is forgiveness, all the way through! We thank you Jesus, with all our heart; and pray in your name, that we never part! We repent from our sins, everyday; and thank you for paying for them, in the ultimate way!

April 3

The truth of Jesus sets us free from sin, through Faith in Him! As we embrace the love of God through Christ Jesus, we have a burning desire to share the good news (Gospel) with all! Let us allow the love of Christ Jesus to speak louder than words, so the doubters can be moved by our authentic kindness! That kindness comes from a relationship with Christ Jesus and by the power of the Holy Spirit of Truth! May the peace of the Lord in us, invite the doubters to know Christ Jesus intimately!

April 4

The fortitude that comes from persevering with courage and strength from faith in the most High God, through Christ Jesus, builds our character with hope! May we encourage others with our steadfast faith in Jesus! May we give all Glory to God, for every good thing in our life! May the old self in us become less, as the new creation in Christ becomes more, in Jesus' mighty name!

April 5

Don't look to the lie of the world for understanding, but go to the truth of God's word through Christ Jesus! Become that which you seek through the Holy Spirit and share the love and hope that comes from Faith in Jesus! Put others before yourself and worry not about their ignorant opinions that are not in compliance with Christ Jesus! Absolutely nothing is more important than our faith in Jesus and the Grace of God through that relationship; that brings refuge from our lost ways! May the peace and love of the Lord rest upon all who have faith in Christ Jesus!

April 6

As temptations knock on the door of our minds, may the Holy Spirit of truth answer it! May we surrender it to God and not allow its entry in us; or it will lead us to torment! The word of God is wisdom and Christ Jesus is the word! As we walk in the yoke with Christ, our walk entertains all that is noble, true, kind, lovely and compassionate! As we allow the word of God to go deeper into us, we become more aware of those things that aren't in compliance with the will of God! We move away from all sin (repent) and guide the willing as well! In Christ Jesus' mighty name, may we continue the good works through faith in the Son of God (Jesus/Yeshua) and finish well!

April 7

The best way we can invite others to know Christ Jesus, is by projecting the love of God unconditionally! For God is love; and Jesus is one with God! Moreover, the love we project through faith in Christ, keeps us in union with the Father and the Son! We become the love we seek, when we take Christ Jesus into our hearts! That's the love that drives out all fear and dominates all darkness! It is the light of the Lord, that comforts the lost with a direction towards perfection, through Christ Jesus!

April 8

If we learn from the world and it is not the truth of God, then we have many issues and beliefs that are erroneous! We must get honest by checking our motives and seeing the part we play in the lie!

As we open ourselves up to the truth of Christ Jesus; He guides us from darkness to light; From lies to truth; From chaos to clarity; From insanity to tranquility; From evil to love! May we embrace the truth that sets us free from all iniquity! In the mighty name of Jesus, we pray!

April 9

Jesus is the Light of the World, who leads us out of darkness! He is the truth, that sets us free from sin! As we embrace Christ Jesus, we set ourselves apart from our sinful nature and embrace our new selves in Christ! We understand a new peace and love through faith in Christ Jesus! We want others to feel the liberation that comes from taking the Son of God into their hearts! Yet those living in darkness, hate the light! Those who use the lie to get ahead, don't want to hear the truth! As disciples of Christ Jesus, we are responsible for leading the sinners to the Prince of Peace! May we all embrace the Grace of God, through faith in Christ Jesus!

April 10

For all that are hungry and thirsty for peace and love, they will be satisfied by taking Christ Jesus into their hearts! Faith in Christ Jesus will suffice for all struggles in this life! He is the way, when we lose our way! As we center ourselves through prayer with Jesus, the Holy Spirit will enlighten us! God sees and hears all things! Trust in the Lord thy God through Christ Jesus! May that which is hidden, be revealed to all that have faith in Christ Jesus!

April 11

As we eat the bread of life and digest the word of God through Christ Jesus, we become one with God! As we drink the blood of Christ Jesus, we become one with the resurrection and eternal life! With a new hope in the life to come and the love of the Lord in our hearts, we share the good news (Gospel) with all who are willing to hear it and receive it! May the power of the Holy Spirit, be upon all who look to share the good news of Christ Jesus!

April 12

Faith in Christ Jesus comes by choosing to believe, instead of doubting! There are many people that have taught lessons of virtue; but there is only one person that is the way, the truth and the life; Jesus is He! He is the light in this world and the next! He is the most authentic love known to anyone! I pray for all those that doubt Him! I pray they choose to receive Him into their hearts and that He saves their souls! For without Jesus, we are just as lost as the doubter!

April 13

The Holy Spirit of truth comes upon us through faith in Christ Jesus! As we allow the Holy Ghost to guide us, we become one with God by emulating His love! Our character is filled with acts of kindness, as well as an altruistic (selfless) mentality and spirit that conveys the love of God to all! May we all be open to receive this precious gift of love from the Holy Spirit; in the mighty name of Jesus Christ!

April 14

In the mighty name of Jesus, we ask for help in bringing the message of hope, that's only found through faith in Jesus, the Son of God! May we speak words empowered by the Holy Spirit of Truth; May those words of truth, open the closed minded! Moreover, may they soften those, whose hearts have been hardened, by life's difficulties! Furthermore, may the words of truth, guide those who have gotten comfortable, in the world's lies! In Christ Jesus' mighty name, we pray!

April 15

Heavenly Father God, in the name of your Son Jesus, I surrender myself to you completely! May I show the peaceful restraint, of a flexible servant, of the most High God! May the negative reactions of others, build my character with love! May I set healthy boundaries, that can speak up, without putting other people down! May I make this day about serving others with altruistic acts of love and eliminate self seeking motives in all its forms! In the precious name of Jesus, I pray!

April 16

The Lord is the light in all darkness and He is the full measure of love! The Lord is quick to forgive, through Faith in Him! Jesus is the Messiah and the Son of the Creator; who is also, one with the Father! No one comes to the Father, but through Him! Don't fight this truth, but embrace it; before it is too late! It's the most beautiful gift ever given and only the ignorant about this truth, can get insulted by this precious gift from God! I pray that all that read this, accept Jesus into their hearts and repent from their sins! In Jesus' mighty name, I pray!

April 17

To be one with God the Father, is to be one with the Son, Jesus the Christ! To know the Father, is to know the generosity of the Son; who shared all of Himself with us! Jesus taught us a spiritual and paradoxical reward; that we never had so much, until we gave it all away! Today in Jesus' mighty name, with His generosity in our hearts, let's be good sharers of love, time, compassion and finances! As we freely received all things from God, let's freely share them with the least among us, in Jesus' mighty name!

April 18

It is Faith in Christ Jesus, that makes the impossible, probable! It is through this Faith, that we are forgiven for all the things we've done wrong! It is through faith in Jesus, that all fear of what might happen, dissipates! There is power in the name of Jesus; and it can do all things, for the one who believes! I pray in the mighty name of Jesus, the Christ, that all those who lack in faith, are transformed by the power of Holy Spirit and take Jesus Christ into their hearts!

April 19

Jesus is the truth of God; and He is the one that can save us from our sinful behavior! For all that choose to deny this truth, they choose darkness over light! To accept Jesus into your heart, is to embrace the truth that sets you free, from the lie of the world and the bondage of sin! I accept Jesus as the Christ; The Son of God; The Messiah! Help me Lord, by the power of the Holy Spirit, to project your love towards everyone that is kind and unkind; so they may know you are my Lord and Savior! In the mighty name of Jesus, I pray!

April 20

My relationship with Jesus the Christ, is the most important relationship in my life! It helps me to be the love I seek in the world and share that love with all that will receive it from me! I share the good news of Jesus, the Son of God, to all who will listen! I pray that the Holy Spirit of Truth, speaks from my mouth to their hearts; and they receive the truth, that will set them free from the wage of sin! May the doubters not deter my efforts or voice pertaining to my faith in the Prince of Peace; Jesus is He! May all who hear the truth of Jesus, embrace his wonderful Grace! In the mighty name of Jesus, I pray for all!

April 21

It is by faith in Christ Jesus, that we persevere through difficulties in this life! When we lean on our own understanding, we cause our own suffering! As we place our hope in the Lord in this life and the next, we free ourselves from all fear! When we look to see what we can give to those in need, all our needs are met! Let's stand in faith, in the midst of chaos; and serve others with the love of Christ Jesus that brings clarity; in Jesus' Holy name!

April 22

May we speak words that build people up and don't tear them down! May we express kindness in the things we do and say! May the love of Christ Jesus, be the light in us, that illuminates the darkness in someone else! May we stand for God's will through His word and not fall for the world's corruption! May we be guided by the Holy Spirit of truth, so we don't guide by the lie of the world and become blind guides! May sharing the love of Jesus the Christ, be our goal for the day! In Jesus' mighty name, we pray!

April 23

As the spiritual birth takes place through faith in Christ Jesus; we as disciples begin each day anew (a new start in a positive way)! We live in the forgiveness of the cross; therefore, we harbor no resentments! We are born again through the Holy Spirit of Truth, that comes into our heart's, from taking Christ Jesus into our lives authentically (genuinely)! This is the way, so we don't lose our way! This is the true Christian, in following Christ Jesus! He is the only way to the Father; in the Kingdom of Light! In Jesus' mighty name, may we guide the lost with a steadfast faith in the Son of God; Jesus is He!

April 24

Jesus is the Light of the World that drives out all darkness! Once we stand in this light of love and feel the peace beyond all understanding; we don't want to go back to the darkness of sin! Yes, we all fall short of the Glory of God; but we strive for righteousness still! To go back to our sinful ways after accepting Jesus into our hearts is a contradiction, that causes torment to our spirits! We may not be good; but we should strive to be! May we be more like Jesus today and less like our sinful selves! In Jesus' mighty name, I pray for all of us!

April 25

To really understand the magnitude of God giving us Jesus to be crucified for the forgiveness of sins; is beyond our human understanding! The pain of this great gift from God, cannot be fathomed! The precious gift from God and the obedience of Christ Jesus, is something I embrace with all my heart, soul, mind and strength! Everyone is welcomed to receive this gift from God, through Faith in Jesus; His only begotten Son! Don't reject this gift; that was the ultimate price paid for our salvation! Today, I receive Jesus Christ as my Lord and Savior! Where I am weak, be my strength Lord! My Hope is in you alone! This hope helps me to persevere with courage and strength! May I live to serve the least among us, in Jesus' mighty name!

April 26

We rejoice in our Lord and Savior Jesus Christ! He has set us free from the wage of sin! We boast about our hope in the Lord and share our love for Him with others! Where we are wicked, He is righteous! Yet, He took our sin upon Himself, so we would be reconciled with the Father of light! How could we not praise Him! Now that we are saved through Faith and not by works; may we share the good news (Gospel) with all! In the mighty name of Jesus!

April 27

We are one with the Father, through His Son! As the Son is one with the Father, so are we through Faith in the Son! Thank you Jesus, for teaching us a new way; so that we could be saved from our destructive ways of thinking and living! Thank you Jesus, for your Holy Sacrifice; that has set us apart from death; and gives us eternal life, through Faith in the Son of God! May we share the good news of your love and truth to all! Be with us and guide our words, as we now live to serve you and not ourselves with selfish ambitions! In Jesus' mighty name, I pray for all of us!

April 28

We have Grace by Faith in Christ Jesus and not by works, so no one can boast! It's a gift from God! That does not give us a pass to continue to sin and manipulate this great gift from God! We may fall short on many levels; but we aspire to live by virtue and not by vice! As we die to self daily; we now live to serve the Lord, and not every evil desire! May we lead by example, so the doubter will be intrigued to know more! May our character let everyone know that we are followers of Christ Jesus; our Lord and Savior! Let's be a blessing from the many lessons in God's word, through faith in His Son Jesus! In Jesus' mighty name, we pray!

April 29

The wage of sin is death; but Faith in Christ Jesus has conquered death! Our human nature is weak, but the Son of God is strong! I don't lean on myself or my own understanding according to the law! I fall short on my own accord! It's only through Faith in Christ Jesus, that I can be saved from my sinful nature! I aspire to live by love in all it's forms; and die to self seeking motives daily! May Jesus become more in me and I become less; as to serve many in Jesus' mighty name!

April 30

When we surrender ourselves to Jesus, we surrender our pride! We no longer look to bring glory to our name, but to the one who saved us from Eternal Damnation! Great things begin to occur when we surrender completely! We no longer make the day and all its activities about us! We become free from self and the opinions of others! We put the least among us, before us, in true humility! Virtue, becomes achievable through authentic love; for our fellow man, woman and child! We don't take insults personally; we detach in loving prayer! We become the peace we seek, through the Holy Spirit of truth, in Jesus' mighty name!

May 1

As I abide in the word of God, I accept Christ Jesus as truth to the lie in this world and the lie in me! As I stand for the truth of God, God stands with me! If God is with me through Faith in His Son, I fear no one and nothing in this life or the next! My hope in the Lord, conquers all fear; and brings a peace beyond all understanding! Let us put our trust in Christ Jesus; who God gave us as a ransom for many, so we could be one with Him FOREVER! In Jesus' mighty name, I pray!

May 2

It's all about the word of God and our motives to bring glory to His name; through faith in His Son, Jesus the Christ! It's also about abiding (to conform to) by the word of God and guiding others to the truth of Christ Jesus, by the power of the Holy Spirit! Furthermore, it's about expressing authentic love, through true humility to the least among us! It's not about selling a dream to the doubters! It's about love, faith, service, generosity and Grace! Let's all be the love of Christ Jesus and search no more! In Jesus' (Yeshua) mighty name, we pray!

May 3

The truth of Christ Jesus, sets all free; who choose to believe, that He is the Son of God! For all those that want to deny this truth, will suffer by the choice they make! How much proof does the blind need to see? How much proof does the deaf need to hear? Truly BLESSED are those that did not see or hear in person, but chose to believe in Jesus the Christ! There is no middle ground for the doubter! You're either with God, through His only begotten Son Jesus or you are not! Don't try to bargain and negotiate with God's truth! The truth that sets you free is Jesus and Jesus alone! There is no other way to the kingdom of light! There's light and there's darkness! Choose Jesus the Light of the World! I pray for the obtuse (slow to understand) doubter, that doesn't understand Grace! May the Holy Spirit of truth, free you from the lie that leads to everlasting death! In Jesus' mighty name, I pray!

May 4

May my focus not be on how others speak to me, but how I respond in a skillful way; that conveys love and understanding! As I keep myself yoked with the Lord, I carry His peace from place to place and from person to person! For as the Lord is good; I aspire to be good! We are called out of all forms of wickedness (sin) through faith in Christ Jesus! As we project the love of the Messiah to all, the Lord gives us refuge from all evil! Fear nothing; because faith in the Lord has conquered all fear!

May 5

It is by Faith in Christ Jesus, that we are pardoned from our sins! It's only by Faith, that we please God; who gave us everything now and what is to come! Although we may have little possessions with Faith, still we have much! It's by Faith, that all great things are possible! Now that we have Faith, may we abide by God's word through Christ Jesus! Let's look past any difficulties in this life, and with Faith in Christ Jesus, find hope for the next life to come! In Jesus' mighty name, we pray!

May 6

How can you hear and not listen? How can you see and not believe? How can you feel and not take it into your heart? The truth of Christ Jesus, enriches every soul that believes in Him! He shows what is important and still the doubters choose to resist! As we embrace His love, our love doesn't run out! We become one with love! Choose the love of God, through His Son, who is one with the Father! Be the light of the Lord, so hope may illuminate the darkness of the doubter! In Jesus' mighty name, share the love and hope of the Lord with all!

May 7

As I rejoice in the Lord, I extend His great love to all! I become that love I seek, by emulating His kindness! As I give of myself generously, with loving humility, my spirit soars to the stratosphere! Christ Jesus, has given us the ultimate gift and sacrifice! Who am I to hold back all that I can give? I am a servant of the most High God, who gives generously to us all, the gift of Grace to the faithful! As I take this wonderful gift, I give all that I am in loving gratitude to everyone! In Jesus' mighty name, I do all things!

May 8

As disciples of Christ Jesus, we need to be patient with the individual who doesn't get it yet! The one who lacks understanding and that authentic connection of love, which brings peace beyond all understanding! It's got to be okay, that they're not there yet. It's about attraction, through the expression of love in all it's forms! It's not about promotion with haste. We who have Faith in the Son of God, know how wonderful Jesus the Christ is; and that nothing is more important than our Faith in Him! Yet we can't force our Faith on anyone, or they might rebel and we lose that opportunity to save a soul! We are to guide those willing to receive the truth of Christ Jesus, with love and the wisdom of God's word! For those not willing to believe in Jesus as the Son of God, we remain patient with their doubt, but we remain steadfast in our Faith in Jesus, the Messiah! In Jesus' mighty name, may we be open to receive the Holy Spirit as our guide, so we can guide the doubters to Christ Jesus!

May 9

Through the surrender of self to God, through faith in Christ Jesus; I have come to the end of self-centeredness and to the beginning of God consciousness! I never had so much love, until I became the principles of love, through emulating Christ Jesus! As I strive to serve and not be served; I become the altruistic love that is one with God and the universe! Therefore, my self-love is no longer about self and what I can accomplish; but what I can give away with love, to help others! In conclusion to a topic that never ends, but can always become more; I say this, that we never had so much, until we gave it all away with love!

May 10

Do not be deceived by anyone's sinful nature! Do not entertain debauchery in your mind, but surrender all difficulties to our Lord Jesus, the Christ; who has defeated sin and makes victory attainable through Faith in Him! Do not associate with those who enjoy sinning, but guide those who want a way out! Share the gospel and you share a solution through Faith in Christ Jesus! Be the light of the Lord and darkness cannot over take you! May Jesus the Christ be with you all, in Jesus' mighty name!

May 11

Let the light of the Lord, illuminate all darkness in your life! May your Faith in Jesus as the Son of God, make all fear in you dissipate! May you see past the pain of your present circumstances, with hope that looks forward to what the Lord has in store for those who love Him! May the peace of the Lord, replace all the self talk that dominates you! May we all let God's word guide us, from chaos to clarity, replacing hate with love and pride with humility! In Christ Jesus' mighty name, we pray!

May 12

May I not look to the world with all it's possessions as fulfillment; but May I look to God's word, through faith in Christ Jesus, as the truth that frees my soul from all iniquity! The love of God fulfills us beyond human understanding! Don't be mislead by the world and all the desires of the flesh that leave people empty in the end! Know Jesus, and you shall know peace! Embrace the Grace of God, through Christ Jesus and know the hope of salvation! Seek the kingdom of God with all your heart, soul, mind and strength and you will find reconciliation with God the Father, through His Son Jesus! May the love of the Lord, be the love you seek, so you search no more! Then in Jesus' loving name, you share that love with the world, to be called children of God!

May 13

Do not be mislead by the temptations of this world, for they will never suffice! Be transformed by the word of God, through Christ Jesus! May your aspirations be propelled by the love you have for God! May our love be expressed in loving service to all our Neighbors! May our character be gentle with the doubter, but firm in our Faith in Christ Jesus! May we embrace the lost with love so they want to know more, instead of pushing them away with discord! In Jesus' mighty name, let's be the light of the Lord, to all lost in darkness!

May 14

This world is filled with trials and tribulation! God has given us a way out and a way through, with His precious Son Jesus as our Savior! We who have faith in Christ, know the peace in chaos and the patience in overcoming difficulties! As we plow through addictions, impulsive and compulsive behavior, obsessive thoughts and many other difficulties, we can find refuge in Christ Jesus, by being in the yoke with Him! We are never alone and can rejoice in all situations! For where we are weak, Christ Jesus is strong! May the love that brings everlasting peace from faith in Christ Jesus, rest upon you always, In Jesus' mighty name!

May 15

Daily prayer

Christ Jesus, be the courage and wisdom in my voice, to those who sow discord! Be the thoughts of virtue in my mind, that gives birth to peace! Be the love of you, extended through me, to help the less fortunate! Be the friend in me, that shows all his foes how to love! Be the generosity in me, that shows the stingy how to share! Be the humility in me, that shows the arrogant how to be humble! Help me to stay in the yoke with you, all the days of my life! In the mighty name of Jesus, I pray!

May 16

The love of God is expressed completely, through His Son Jesus! He held nothing back, in His gift to us! He gave us the most valuable, precious and excruciatingly painful gift! Furthermore, the gift didn't stop there! As we repent of our sins and take Jesus into our hearts, we are given many other gifts from our salvation through Faith! God is the most loving and generous God! How could we not be grateful? How could we not want to give back? Do not let the lost guide you, in their erroneous beliefs! Let the truth of Christ Jesus and His Holy Sacrifice, set you free from all lies! Return the love of God, to the least among us, with loving gratitude! We have been given much and much we should want to give! May the generosity of God's love, speak through our compassion for one another! In Jesus' mighty name!

May 17

To put on the body of Christ, is to be love in all it's forms! To be quick to serve, listen, forgive and be kind in a generous way! To be like Jesus, the Son of God, is to aspire to do great things in His name! Bringing Glory and honor to Him, who saved us all, from the wage of sin, through Faith! As we die to selfishness, in every way! We are born anew in an altruistic (selfless) way; being the essence of humility, we put the least before ourselves, in loving service! With great joy, we give back to God, by loving one another, without hidden motives for self! In Jesus' mighty name, let's be the love of God today, through faith in Christ Jesus!

May 18

The more I surrender myself to the Lord, the more peace I have! The more I give away to others, the more I gain in the spirit of truth! The more I serve the least among us, the less I need! There are many rewards, in the gift of giving, that surpass anything, one might receive here on earth! As we emulate the love of Christ Jesus, wholeness and peace become our shadow from the Lords great light! We never had so much, until we gave it all away! Let's look to serve others, as Jesus served us, in His mighty name!

May 19

I preach to reach and I connect to teach! May the Holy Spirit of truth, through Christ Jesus, guide every word to the heart and soul of those listening! May my character match my words or I will lose credibility with people and they will turn away from the truth! May I be patient with those who mock me, for they know not what they do! May I guide the doubter with patience, so that they will seek more! May I rejoice with my brothers and sisters in Christ, so that which is difficult alone, becomes a celebration of Faith with many! As we become one vine with Christ Jesus, let's project His love through us, to serve many! In Jesus' mighty name, I pray for all!

May 20

Death could not hold Christ Jesus, because He is the truth of God! He is the Messiah and anyone who puts their faith in Him, shall live and never die! Jesus is one with the breath of life and nothing evil dwells in His glorious light of love! He is one with the FATHER of all creation! To love Christ Jesus, is to love the FATHER! To be loved by Christ Jesus, is to be loved by the FATHER! To know Christ Jesus, is to know the FATHER! May Jesus, in His Holy name, guide the lost to Him, as the Great Shepherd, for all His lost sheep!

May 21

Our joy for the day comes from the positive projection of Christ Jesus in our future before we arrive! Our hope is in the Lord and not in ourselves! We are optimistic in our Faith, in the Son of God! We look past all difficulties, with great joy in our hearts! We see trials as opportunities to grow in character and strengthen our Faith in Christ Jesus! May we all persevere with courage and strength that comes from Faith in God, through His Son Jesus! In Jesus' mighty name, we pray for all!

May 22

As children of God and saved by Faith in Christ Jesus, we have an obligation to spread the good news to all! We share the love of Christ, through good works for the poor; and by being kind, to those who are not! Sharing what we have, with those that don't have anything! Speaking words of encouragement, to those who are discouraged! Our character speaks louder than words! We study the word of God, to share the truth! We stand for the truth of Christ Jesus and we don't fall for the lie of the flesh! May the Holy Spirit of Truth, be yoked with us always, as we proclaim the good news of Christ Jesus to all! In Jesus' mighty name, we pray!

May 23

Many have suffered much to bring the good news of Christ Jesus to the world; and what faith in Him brings to those who repent from their sins, and believe in their hearts, that Jesus is the Son of the living God! God knows we all fall short of His Glory! That's why Jesus came into the world and took the wage of sin upon Himself as a ransom for many, so we could be forgiven! Furthermore, we all have a sinful nature in the flesh; but through faith in Jesus as the Messiah, we are reconciled with the Father! All Glory belongs to God the Father and His benevolent Son Jesus, who are one love and light in the Kingdom of God! Let's embrace the Grace of God through faith in Christ Jesus! For many have paid the ultimate price for us to be where we are in our faith and understanding of our Lord and Savior Jesus! Thank you to all known and unknown brothers and sisters of Christ, who paid the ultimate sacrifice! We love you and will return the kindness by bringing the good news everywhere we go! In Jesus' mighty name, we ask God our Father for the fortitude to convey His message of hope to the world!

May 24

Our goal for the day, is to share the good news (Gospel) of Christ Jesus, by being the love of God! We speak about Jesus in character, by emulating the Prince of Peace in every way! We share the Gospel with all and go to great lengths for those who want to learn more! Our goal is to bring faithful servants to Christ Jesus, so they may be saved by the Grace of God! Our goal is not about accumulating stuff in the world for ourselves! May we be the light of the Lord to all, in Jesus' wonderful name!

May 25

When you want to act out to injustice, and hurt the people hurting you or the ones you love, remember how God handled the crucifixion, of His loving Son Jesus! We are to emulate that love and patience that God showed us! We trust God in all situations, and His love and judgement is sufficient, in all trials, tribulations and tragedies! Faith is more than belief; it's trusting that which we cannot see! God, I trust you with every situation in my life and all those I hold dear! Furthermore, I trust you with my life and the lives that are precious to me! In Jesus' mighty name, I pray that we all have Faith in God; and that we trust Him in all situations!

May 26

When people try to coax (persistently persuade) you into an argument or fight, resist in the name of Jesus! When people attack your character, know that you are a new creation, through Faith in Christ Jesus! Stay in the clarity of God's word and don't fall for the lie of the world! No one's opinion is the truth of God! We stand for the truth of Jesus! Remember the righteousness of God's Son Jesus and how he endured the worst for our sins! Lets emulate that fortitude, that perseveres with courage and strength, that comes from faith in God! We rejoice in the times of trials, for it improves our character, through Faith in Christ Jesus! May we all find peace in the mist of chaos, through Jesus Christ! In Jesus' mighty name, I pray for His light, to triumph over all darkness!

May 27

As we stay in the light of Christ Jesus, truth becomes our mission in life! The Son of God is truth and Christ Jesus is He! Nothing evil is welcomed in the Kingdom of Light; but all are welcome to repent from evil and to take Christ Jesus into their hearts and make Him their Lord and Savior! He is the only way, when we lose our way! He is the only truth that really matters in this world and the next! No one can come to the Father, except through Him! Do not be deceived from the doubters of this truth! They will kneel and confess this truth one day! In Jesus' mighty name, I pray that all that read this, agree with the truth of Christ Jesus and that truth sets them free from all iniquity!

May 28

We are called to be righteous, as God the Father is righteous! We may fall short on many levels, but we strive each and every moment, of every day! Christ Jesus intercedes on our behalf, through faith in Him! As we repent and move away from sin; we aspire towards all that is noble, true, lovely, kind and of every virtue that does the will of God! As we stay yoked to the Lord, no evil can overcome us! For we don't stand alone in darkness, but together we stand in the light and love of Christ Jesus! In the mighty name of Jesus, I pray that we all submit to the truth of God!

May 29

Now that we are saved by Faith in Christ Jesus; may the Holy Spirit sanctify our minds and bodies! We participate in this sanctification, by living with the love of Christ in our hearts, minds and spirits! We don't bargain and negotiate with any form of sin! Sin becomes repulsive to the spirit, when the love of God, through Christ Jesus is in us! We may fall short of the glory of God daily; but our hearts aspire to live by the word of God! This transformation is seen by many, who don't recognize the character in us, that is expressed through loving kindness! All Glory to God, who enlightens us daily, through the Holy Spirit of Truth! Let's bring GLORY to God, by emulating the love of Christ Jesus to all! In Jesus' mighty name, I pray for all!

May 30

How can I express my love for you Jesus? Serve the least among you with love! How can I give to you Lord? Forgive one another! How can I be with you God? Have Faith in my Son Jesus, who is one with the Father! What should I do to be called your son? Love your neighbor as yourself! We are to share all that we have, on the inside and outside; with loving Faith in Jesus, that puts others before ourselves! In Jesus' mighty name, give us the fortitude, to serve all, in your loving name!

May 31

To know true contentment in all situations, is to know Christ Jesus intimately in your heart! To be grateful in prayer before ones request, is to trust God through His loving Son! To meditate on virtues, is to yearn for righteousness! May our efforts to emulate the Messiah, bring Glory to God, as we serve one another with loving compassion! In Jesus' mighty name, I pray!

June 1

We must resist the temptations in this world, as obedient children of God, through Faith in Christ Jesus! As we put others before ourselves, in all humility; we bring Glory to God, by emulating His only begotten Son Jesus! When our motives are not for profit in any form, we emulate the Messiah! Our Father, who Art in Heaven, sees all things and blesses those, who share with the least among us! In Jesus' mighty name, let's see what we can give, instead of what we can get in this life!

June 2

Every time we express love in one form or another, we embrace God through that expression! God is love; therefore, the love given with no hidden motives, becomes one with God! Jesus is the gift of love from God! Jesus taught us the value of love above all else in this world! When we put love first, for God, through His altruistic Son, we are perfected through Faith in the Son and His love for us! We are to extend that same love to one another; regardless of the other persons behavior! We may not like what people do, but we are now son's and daughters of the most High God through faith in Christ Jesus; and we are the branches of love from the one true Vine! In Jesus' mighty name, may we put the love of God above all else today!

June 3

The chaos of anger can be overwhelming at times! Actions and overreactions can be extremely confusing to most of us! Yet we don't have to participate in this destructive behavior in any way. We can surrender all things to Christ Jesus and find the strength to endure this difficult emotion, that's being directed at us. The love of Christ, is patient and slow to anger! The love of Christ, overcomes all hostility! The light of the Lord, guides us in times of darkness! The Prince of Peace, brings harmony back into our life when we forgive others of their wrong doings! May the Grace of God, through Faith in Christ Jesus, rest upon all who are facing trials and tribulations from others today! In Jesus' mighty name, we pray for all!

June 4

All we need and more, is in Christ Jesus! As I rest in you oh Lord, my peace grows in every situation! I look forward to being with you in the next life and serving you in this one! I love you with all my heart, mind, soul and strength! In surrendering all to you, I want for nothing! My joy is sharing the good news (Gospel) to all who will receive it! Through faith in you Lord, there is life after death; and in that Grace there is liberation from the wage of sin! In Jesus' mighty name, may I serve others before myself!

June 5

We look to serve and not be served, with the love of Christ Jesus! We boast only about what Jesus has done for us! If any pride be in us, may it be in serving the least among us, in Jesus' loving name! May everything we do, bring Glory to God's name and not our own! May others be attracted to the kindness we express, so they want to know more about our faith in Christ Jesus! The attraction is in our character and the promotion is in the love we express to everyone! Let's be the light of the Lord, in someone's darkness today; in Jesus' mighty name!

June 6

I speak to you, and you hear my cry oh Lord! I read your word, and it comforts me! I pray to you, and you answer me! Your word is alive in me, and no one can stop your love that flows through me! I want all to know you intimately! You are my God; and in you, I am well pleased! Your love Jesus, is the truth that sets me free! In your love there is no darkness! I refrain from all sin, so I can bask in your light oh Lord! I fall short daily, but you forgive me and guide me by the power of the Holy Spirit! As I serve others, I feel thee! In Jesus' mighty name, may I lay down all I hold dear, for the least among us!

June 7

Amazing Grace!

Absolutely Amazing Love! What a gift of love (Jesus dying on the cross for the forgiveness of sins)! Thank you God for your forgiveness! May my Faith in your Son Jesus please you! I love you God!

May the love for your Son, be expressed by the love I give to all, in Jesus' loving name! May I give the Grace (forgiveness) that I embrace to others!

By the power of the Holy Spirit, guide me in this love to serve all; In Jesus' mighty name, I pray!

June 8

In Jesus' Holy name, help us keep your light in our minds and Satan's darkness out! Filter each thought through the Holy Spirit of truth, so that we don't fall for the lies in this world and are in compliance with your will for our lives! May we look to bring Glory to your name and not our own; as we serve all those in need! In Jesus' mighty name, we pray!

The truth of God is Christ Jesus! That truth defies all logic! God makes the impossible happen! Let these facts fill your mind and increase your faith!

June 9

Heavenly Father, we thank you for all that you do! How you take evil and transform it into righteous acts of kindness! Through your Son Jesus, we learn to transform hate into love and chaos into clarity! We go from falling for the lie of this world, to standing for the truth of your word, by the power of the Holy Spirit! As we are transformed by your Holy word, we put others before ourselves, and make the day about serving all, in Jesus' mighty name!

June 10

From the moment I awake, to the time I go to sleep, may I be in Holy Surrender! I see when my pride, lust, greed, anger and all forms of sin wants to tempt me and take me away from the will of God in my mind! I've gotten better at spotting this sinful thought process that takes place; and not bargaining or negotiating with it! Only Holy Surrender to God through Christ Jesus will suffice (be enough) against these temptations! I pray in Jesus' mighty name, that where I am weak, Christ Jesus' strength is perfected in me!

June 11

To authentically serve others, with no hidden motives for glory or gain, is the will of God for our lives! To love others because of who you are with Christ Jesus, is to be one with God! May we emulate the will of God today, by surrendering ourselves in Faith to Christ Jesus! In Jesus' Holy name, may we continue to pray for all!

Words of warning/instruction:
Do not follow the unfaithful in their folly! Resist all temptation and be the example of righteousness to those lost in darkness!

June 12

We who know Yeshua, have a burning desire to guide and serve all with the truth of Christ Jesus; and to embrace that truth with the doubter, is a goal we strive for with patience! We feel the freedom from that truth; and we want to share it with all! Some will doubt and others will mock us! It's okay for them to be wrong today! They don't get it yet! There was a time we didn't get it! May they see the light of our Lord and Savior, by how we express our love, while serving all, in Jesus' Holy name!

June 13

If what is true to you, has you standing with the lies of this world (faithless); then we must concede that only Jesus is truth in this world and the next! Therefore, to thine own self be true, is erroneous to the truth of God! For no one is the truth of God, except Christ Jesus! His truth is love in all its forms; and its authentic in every way! To that truth is what we are called to be! In Jesus' mighty name!

Things to remember:
    Lean not on your own understanding, but on every word that comes from Christ Jesus!

June 14

When we think of being obedient to God, as something difficult; think about the lamb of God, who has taken the sins of the world, upon His sinless self, through much suffering, so we could be FORGIVEN, through Faith in Him! When something seems unreasonable, by being obedient to the will of God, remember how Jesus, took unreasonable suffering, for the reason of forgiveness, for our sinful nature! May we thank God daily; by striving to be righteous; in Christ Jesus' loving name!

June 15

To have faith in Christ Jesus, is to remain in the light of hope, when difficult times come into our life! Through faith in the Son of God, we can persevere through anything life gives us! Our strength comes from knowing the truth about the Messiah; and that truth sets us free in this life and the next! May we serve others with this hope in the Lord, so they may see past their present circumstances! In Jesus' mighty name, we pray!

June 16

Lord, I am a lost man without you! Through faith in you Jesus, I am filled with the Holy Spirit, to bring the good news of the Gospel to all! It's by Faith, that all things come into fruition; of myself, I fall short of the glory of God! I strive for righteousness and fall short everyday; but my Faith in you, saves me from the law I can't fulfill! I am so grateful to you God, that I propel forward with enthusiasm about the good news of salvation, through Faith in your Son, Jesus the Christ! I share this as a feast, among starving people for the truth! Some refuse to eat the word of God and starve! Others can't get enough and want to share what's been given! There's plenty that comes from you oh God! May we invite all to dine with us on the body of Christ Jesus; so the word can be alive in us and expressed through the loving service, that we provide for the poor in spirit! In Jesus' mighty name, I pray!

June 17

To know the truth of Christ Jesus, is to sustain us from sin, through Faith! When we are one with God, through faith in His Son, we are one with the Holy Spirit! When we entertain sin, it has a powerful pull on us! When we live contrary to the spirit, as children of the most High God, through Faith in Christ Jesus, we know torment! Knowing what we know now about the Son of God, means we can't deceive ourselves and act like we don't know! We stand for the spirit and surrender our flesh! It's no longer about us, but about serving the Lord, through love and acts of kindness to all in need! In Jesus' mighty name, may we deny ourselves and serve the Lord in spirit!

June 18

It's through Faith in Christ Jesus, that what we hope for will come into fruition! God has set us aside as His faithful children; and if God is with us, no one and nothing can stand against us! Our hope is the positive projection of God's protection (refuge)! Christ Jesus, has made us victorious over sin, through Faith in Him! May we see past the pain of this life; and with great hope in our hearts, persevere through all trials and tribulations! May all our hope be in the Lord, and not in ourselves, in Jesus' mighty name!

June 19

We are saved by Faith in Christ Jesus! Now that we know this truth, we share it with all! Not everyone will accept this as the truth; for they have been mislead by the lost! They live in agreement with others, who believe in the erroneous doctrines! They are appalled at us, for sharing the truth about the Messiah! Christ Jesus is He! We tell others that we must all repent for our sins, take Christ Jesus into our hearts, and make Him our Lord and Savior! Yet many are offended at this offer of salvation! We must persist with the truth of the Gospel! Better for one to be saved and hated by many, than none at all! In Jesus' mighty name, may we have the courage to guide the lost to Christ Jesus!

June 20

As I accept the truth of God, through faith in Christ Jesus; I am set free from the lie in me! The word of God is alive in me, and is expressed with loving humility towards all! I am now a servant of the most High God! I put others before myself; and I put to death all forms of selfishness with hidden motives! My love for the Lord, is expressed in how I serve the least among us daily! May the Holy Spirit of truth, speak through my actions, before my words! In Jesus' mighty name, I pray!

June 21

As we reflect on the truth of the Holy Gospel, about Jesus the Son of God, we rejoice in our spirits about salvation! We are one family in God's kingdom of light! Our bloodline is Faith in the lamb of God, who takes away the sins of the world! The realization of this great gift is astonishing! As children overjoyed with a wonderful present; we share this gift with everyone! Our gratitude towards the Messiah, is expressed with a contagious love! The message of hope in Christ Jesus, is infectious to all who are open to receive it! In Jesus' mighty name, let's be an extension of God's love, through Faith in Christ Jesus!

June 22

When I look to you with faith God, you're always there to guide me! Your love is never ending and your wisdom no one can understand! Help me to be obedient in all my ways and to serve the least among us! May I never question you in anyway; but trust you with all things, through Christ Jesus your Son! Where your light is, no darkness can be found! May I meditate on your love all day long; and share it with everyone! For your love is expressed through Christ Jesus; my Lord and Savior! That love is the truth; that sets us all free! In Jesus' mighty name, help me to be the love, that brings clarity into someone's confusion; and the light of compassion, into someone suffering in darkness!

June 23

May we have the kind of compassion that goes into someone's suffering and feels the pain of their loss; without getting lost! Furthermore, let us guide them out gently with patience! As we sit in this pain with them, we will become aware of unresolved pain from our own past! At this time we surrender all that we know and don't know to our Creator through Christ Jesus; who doesn't lack in understanding and compassion! The one thing that expresses compassion better than anything else is our love! May our love comfort those who are lost in their suffering and work as a compass to guide them back to acceptance with peace! In Jesus' loving name, we pray!

June 24

As I speak to the unbeliever, I must not conform to their erroneous beliefs, so we will be in agreement, to avoid conflict! Jesus Christ is the Son of God! There is no lying in Him, for He is the truth! If He said it, that settles it! He sacrificed everything for our forgiveness and still people get insulted when you guide them, to Him! He healed every disease, made the blind see, the dumb talk, the deaf hear, the cripple walk, fed 5000 with 2 fish and 5 loaves of bread, Rose the Dead, died for the sins of the world, so that all would be forgiven through faith in Him; and beat the Wage of Sin, by being raised up on the third day from being dead! He did much more than this! He is pure love and wisdom! Take Yeshua/Jesus into your heart today; for He took you into His, in the very beginning of time! Don't debate about the truth of Christ Jesus; just be obedient to his word, through faith in Him; and He will show you the way, through the Holy Spirit of Truth! In Jesus' mighty name, may all that read this, BELIEVE!

June 25

The generosity of the Lord, is inspired by love and not by works! The light of the Lord, comforts those lost in darkness! He is the refuge, for the abused! The peace of the Lord, dissipates all chaos! For those who seek Christ Jesus, they will be comforted! All that have faith in the Son of God, will be saved from the wage of sin! How great thou art, no one knows; yet you value all with the same love! I am humbled by your majestic power! May I serve thee all the days of my life, by expressing your word to all who will receive it! In Jesus' mighty name, I pray!

June 26

For all that live by the law and not by faith in Christ Jesus, are missing out on God's promise of salvation! No one is justified with God on their own accord! We all need Christ Jesus, and we all need to be saved! Surrender your thinking of another way! There is no other way! Christ Jesus is the way, and the only way! If there was another way, He who is truth, would have told us! In Jesus' mighty name, may we all stand together in Faith; and not fall for all the erroneous options in the world!

June 27

Surrender all that is not the will of God, and Do not bargain and negotiate with any form of sin! In all your ways acknowledge Christ Jesus; as the only way to the truth, that sets you free forever! For He is one with God! All that know Him, know the Father as well! May all our motives be about bringing Glory and Honor to God the Father; through faithful acts of kindness, by emulating the love of Christ Jesus! In Jesus' mighty name, let's project all that is good in our faith to everyone!

June 28

As we work towards humility, we surrender ourselves completely, in Jesus' Holy name! We aspire to serve and not be served! We become one with the Father, through Faith in His Son! As we emulate the love of Christ Jesus, we become servants to all! Love and humility are one with God! May we all look to see what we can give to each other, in Jesus' loving name!

Remember that faith with works, serves all those in need, with help!

June 29

May I be quick to listen to the Lord, and may His Commandments be etched into my heart! May I carry love from place to place, with acts of kindness in His mighty name! May my faith in Christ Jesus not falter, in times of distress! Now that I know Grace through Faith; may I hold no grudges towards anyone! May the light of the Lord rest upon me, to serve others and not myself! In Jesus' Holy name, may these words patch the emptiness, in those that are suffering!

June 30

The word of God, is a compass, to all who are lost! The Son (Jesus) of God, is the way, for all those, that lost their way! Worldly possessions, are the tempting lie of this world! Christ Jesus, is the truth in this world and the next! Do not be deceived by the erroneous beliefs of the lost! Jesus is the only way to the Father! In Jesus' Holy name, may the lost be found through faith in the Messiah! Christ Jesus, is He!

July 1

God is the love that doesn't run out! He is the light in this world and the next! He is the king to the Prince of Peace! They are one family of love, that drives out all fear! Jesus is the essence of love, that overcomes all adversity! The love of the Lord, is waiting for all to embrace it; and know true fulfillment, in the light of love! In Jesus' loving name, I pray that all who read this, embrace the love of God, through Faith in His Son!

July 2

The truth of our Lord, is peace! The light of our Lord, is love! The hand of our Lord, is gentle and kind! The eyes of our Lord, are compassionate! The ears of our Lord, are empathetic! The mouth of our Lord, speaks wisdom in every way! All that is good comes from Christ Jesus, our Lord and Savior! May we all take the Lord into our hearts, in Jesus' mighty name!

July 3

The compassion of our Lord, is like a gentle stream of living water, that glistens in the sunlight; It comforts all of us, deep down in our soul! The generosity of our Lord, is the gift of life, from His last breath! Christ Jesus, is the love we have all been searching for! To embrace the love of Christ, is to resist all that is evil! For the love of God is good and the Son of man, is one with God! In Jesus' Holy name, may we emulate the love that comforts all those that are lost and suffering!

July 4

It's the love of Christ Jesus that sets us free; from the hate in the world and the lie in me! His love is truth; and in that truth, is light for all to see! The day we take Christ Jesus into our hearts and repent from our sins, is our Independence Day! Free from being a slave to sin! We thank you God, for your Spirit that came down from Heaven, in thy Son; and taught all of us, the way, the truth and the life to come, through faith in Christ Jesus! May we celebrate, by being extensions of thy love to all! In Jesus' mighty name, we pray to be in compliance with thy will always!

July 5

We are to conform to Christ Jesus and His generous love; that is expressed with deep compassion for the lost and suffering! Living by every virtue and dying to all selfishness! If we wouldn't do it in front of God, then don't do it! Don't bargain or negotiate with any form of sin, or it will have its way with you; leading to death, for a short time of pleasure and long suffering to follow! Don't be tormented, by living contrary to the will of God! Hold fast to the commandments of our Lord and Savior Christ Jesus; and you will become the love and peace you seek in the world! For the world will fail you; but in Christ Jesus you will be fulfilled!

July 6

As we get into the yoke with Christ Jesus, we enter into the love within that yoke; in that love is peace and in that yoke we remain! We take that yoke of love everywhere we go! All that comes our way, we can now learn how to handle with the Lord; because He takes the heaviness of it all on Himself! On our own accord, we are lost and filled with difficulties! With Christ Jesus, all things become possible! In Jesus' mighty name, may we all stay in the yoke with Christ Jesus; and never take it off!

July 7

When we are in the yoke with Jesus, there is light and no darkness can enter it! Staying with Christ, is to move toward virtue and away from sin! To leave the yoke without Jesus, is to negotiate with sin; and sin will overtake us all! Let's not bargain with sin and torment ourselves in the end; instead let's strive toward every good thing that the Lord desires for our lives! In Jesus' mighty name, may we emulate the light and love that comes from God to all of us, through His Son Jesus!

July 8

When you see the light through Christ Jesus, enter it and don't look back to your lost ways in darkness (sin)! Come to the Lord, one and all! For in His light is love; that brings peace into every situation! The Lord of Light drives out all darkness! Surrender yourselves to the Lord and you will lack in nothing! All that you desire in the flesh is fleeting; but in the Spirit of God, through Faith in Christ Jesus, you will know fulfillment! May the light of the Lord, rest upon the faithful forever, in Jesus' mighty name!

July 9

As I put on the love of Christ Jesus, evil can't have its way with me; for the love of our Lord is light and no darkness from this world or the next can extinguish it! As I spread the good news of our Lord and Savior, my character becomes a compassionate love to all! I am responsible for the planting of love, through faith in the Son of God, and I leave the rest to God! For my faith is steadfast and I don't debate about the truth of Christ Jesus! He is and I am through Him, the love I always searched for! Yet, what kind of love would I be, if I didn't share it with everyone? The love from me comes from Christ; and is given, not earned! I may not like what you do, but God's love is more powerful than any sinner! We must be the light of love in all darkness, through Christ Jesus; the light of this world and the next! In Jesus' mighty name, let's be the love of Christ Jesus and search no more! Then love will not elude us, but become our shadow, from His Great Light!

July 10

The Lord is merciful and His love is never ending! All Glory to God the Father, who gave us all, His most precious Son Jesus! Take the truth of that gift into your heart, and may the Holy Spirit of Truth guide you! May your faith in Christ Jesus, propel you to do many kind works for the less fortunate! In Jesus' mighty name, may we return the kindness to the Father, by loving one another!

Let's Remember, we never had so much love, until we gave someone all of ours!

July 11

There is one message of hope and one promise of reconciliation with God the Father; which is only possible through one name! That name is Jesus (Yeshua)! He is the Son of God, who took the sins of the world upon Himself for our Salvation! Those that believe in His name, are set free from the wage of sin; and its eternal damnation! As we repent from our sins, and take Jesus the Christ into our hearts, we experience a hope beyond worldly things; and freedom for our souls! There is no lie in Him, that took our sins! Take that truth into your heart and let that truth set you free forever! In Jesus' mighty name, I pray for the doubters and all the ones mislead; May they see the truth in Jesus; and may they embrace it forever!

July 12

Jesus, Your word is love; and knows no bounds! Nothing can stand in the way of the truth! All will know that you are the Christ, who is one with the Father! Through Faith in you Jesus, we can feel confident in approaching the kingdom of light; where the book of life has our names! The Father welcomes us through you and you alone! What awaits us, gives us strength to endure all things with a joyful heart and a gentle soul! In Jesus' mighty name, may we be the love of Christ to all!

July 13

The negative projection of what might happen, is erroneous to what God wants to happen! Don't let your self talk dominate you and create unnecessary stress! Too much negative self talk, creates anxiety and insanity! Talk to God and surrender yourself completely to God through faith in Christ Jesus! Find hope in His word and let that set you free from the bondage of self! As we serve others with an altruistic heart, we know liberation on a whole new level!

July 14

For the Word of God is life; and the creation of everything we see, hear and feel, that was brought forth by that Word, is good! For the word, and God, are one! The Word is Jesus the Christ; and Through Him is life! Rejoice in this truth and share the good news (Gospel) with all! Share it in a loving way, that emulates the truth of God, through faith in His Son! In Jesus' mighty name, may we be one with the Word to know God, through the Son!

July 15

As we come to you, God, through Faith in your Son Jesus; we are moved from remorse, to loving forgiveness; that gives birth to liberation and hope! The Salvation that comes from faith in you Jesus; motivates us to share this great gift from God! We are ambitious with hope in the Lord and our motives are altruistic in nature! In Jesus' mighty name, may we put others before ourselves, to serve the Lord with a humble heart! May the joy of salvation, be our motivation, to bring the good news to the lost and suffering doubters!

July 16

The birth of our Lord, is the death of our sins! For He who was without sin, has come into this sinful world, as a Holy sacrifice, pleasing to God the Father! Jesus, the Son of God, has taken our wrong doings (sins) upon Himself, so that we may be forgiven through faith in Him! As we repent from our sins and take Jesus into our hearts as our Lord and Savior, we are born again as a new creation through Christ Jesus! This is the ultimate gift from God; and nothing is more Holy or precious! In Jesus' mighty name, we thank God for this tremendous gift, by sharing the good news (Gospel) with all!

July 17

We, who are blind on our own accord; can not lead the blind, without the Light of God! Christ Jesus is that Light! We who lack much and can do little; need to yoke ourselves to Yeshua/Jesus who doesn't lack in anything; and He can do all the things we need; through faith in Him! Now that we see through faith in Christ Jesus, and by the power of the Holy Spirit; let's guide others to the truth of God! Christ Jesus is the Truth! In Jesus' loving name, we pray and meditate on the word of God! Christ Jesus is the word!

July 18

The Lord guides us with His word and the wise follow it with joy! The fool tries to punch holes in the truth, to avoid guilt from their lies! Christ Jesus is truth and His word restores all that is broken in us! There is life in the Lord for all those that believe in Him! Do not entertain what the lost believe, but reject every form of sin! Do not sway with the wind of sin in this world, but look with hope, for the sunlight of the spirit, in the world to come! In Jesus' mighty name, let's live by examples of virtues and not by vice!

July 19

May the peaceful restraint of the Lord be upon me, as my enemies plot against me! May the mercy afforded me through faith in Christ Jesus, help me to be more compassionate! May I be content in who God created me to be; and use that to help others! May I put others before myself, as Christ did for all of us! May I remain humble when I succeed and share the proceeds with those in need! The love of the Lord, is an action word, that brings much kindness into every situation! In Jesus' loving name, may we express loving kindness to the lost and less fortunate!

July 20

May our Lord and Savior Jesus the Christ be with us always; to help guide us in serving others and not ourselves! May we stay grateful for all that the Prince of Peace has sacrificed for our salvation! May the magnitude of God's love through Christ Jesus, propel us forward to share the love of God with everyone! May our focus be of virtue, in guiding others from vice! May our motives be about bringing GLORY to God and not ourselves! In Jesus' mighty name, let's meditate on all the ways love can be expressed today!

July 21

May we emulate the love of Christ Jesus, by being humble amongst one another! May we never look to out do one another; but to support each other with God's will! As Christ laid down His life for us, we are to do the same for each other! As we put others before ourselves, we become children of God! In Jesus' loving name, may we look to serve and not be served!

July 22

The truth of our Lord, is good!
The light of our Lord, is love!
The hand of our Lord, is gentle and kind!
The eyes of our Lord, are compassionate!
The ears of our Lord, are empathetic!
The mouth of our Lord, speaks wisdom in every way!
All that is good comes from Christ Jesus, our Lord and Savior!
May we all take the Lord into our hearts, in Jesus' mighty name!

July 23

We all have struggles in this life! Some are real; and some come from negative thoughts that are defeating us! There is one who has defeated this sinful world and all its difficulties! Christ Jesus is the way when we lose our way; in what is real and what is perceived real! He is the truth to all lies in this world and in our minds! Jesus has conquered sin in all it's forms; and is the life everlasting! Bring Jesus into your heart and know true peace beyond all understanding! May we all submit to the truth of Christ Jesus; and stop fighting ourselves and others! In the mighty name of Jesus, I pray for every person struggling and suffering!

July 24

As we repent from our sins and take Christ Jesus into our hearts, the law of God, is etched into our hearts! The Holy Spirit of truth, reveals every lie in us and in the world! We can no longer remain silent to the doubter; for the truth of Christ Jesus has been revealed to our spirit! We embrace the truth of Christ Jesus, like a mother embraces a child! We love the truth of Christ Jesus and that truth sets us free! In Jesus' mighty name, may we share the good news about the Son of God with everyone!

July 25

The love of Christ Jesus is a fire in me that nothing can extinguish! It propels me forward to seek His truth and to surrender my lie! The word of God is alive and vibrant in my soul! I share the truth of Christ Jesus with great joy for all to know the love of God, that drives out all fear! When we embrace the truth of Christ Jesus, peace becomes our shadow! In Jesus' mighty name, may we stop fighting everyone and everything! May we all become peacemakers and not peace takers! To be one with Christ Jesus, is to know the love that brings peace!

July 26

May the peace and love of our Lord and Savior fill our hearts; so we are compelled to serve others, instead of looking for love to fill us! May we become the love of the Lord, so we search no more! May God use this time to help us grow in love! May the courage and strength that comes from our faith in Jesus, help us to persevere through this difficult time! May the character in us, grow towards the Lord; and bring us and others hope! In Jesus' mighty name, we pray!

July 27

May I speak your truth Lord, bringing Glory to your name and not my own; for in your name is truth; and in mine, there is not! Christ Jesus is truth and in Him, there is no lie! May we who seek truth, follow the light from darkness! Christ Jesus is light; and in Him, there is no darkness! In Jesus' mighty name, may we stand for the truth of Jesus; and follow His light, as we guide others out of the lies of darkness in this world!

July 28

When a person takes Christ Jesus into their heart, they receive the Holy Spirit of TRUTH! In that truth, they are compelled to share the truth with the doubter; so the doubter will know what they know, about Salvation, through Faith in Christ Jesus! Us believers would rather be hated by all and help some be saved; than do nothing at all! We believe with all our hearts that Jesus is the only way to the FATHER; and we choose to share that good news with all! It's not about you thinking like we think, or us being better than you; it's about you being saved from eternal damnation! That's our motive! To help you know Jesus, the Son of God, who takes away the sins of the world! Don't continue to defend your erroneous beliefs! Surrender yourself to Jesus! It's the GREATEST thing us believers have ever done in this life and as brothers and sisters through Christ Jesus, we will celebrate together in Heaven, in our next life! We choose to share God's Grace with all! In Jesus' mighty name, we pray that you take Christ Jesus into your heart and repent!

July 29

Heavenly Father,

Fill us with the Holy Spirit of Truth, in Jesus' mighty name! May we be filled with your love, so we search no more! May we share your love with all; so all know you, through us!

Your truth is love and it saves all from the lie in the world!

There is no fear in your love! Your love is light and it eliminates all darkness! May the positive projection of your love, be our goal for this day! May it be freely given, as you freely give! In Jesus' loving name, let's all emulate the love of God today!

July 30

Heavenly Father,

We come to you in Jesus' Holy name and we thank you for what you created in us and in the world! We put you before the world, since you created it! Please forgive us for all the sins that we have committed! Release us from the guilt of our past and the fear of our future! Perfect your strength in our weakest moments, so that we may have the power to carry out your will! May we always look to bring GLORY to your Holy name; for you are the Creator and we are the creation; anything that is good in us, comes from you! May we use what you give us, to serve others and not ourselves!

In Jesus' mighty name, we pray!

July 31

May we Surrender and be obedient to the word of God, through Christ Jesus! As we embrace the love of God, through His Son; we see the gift of Grace in all its forms and persevere with great joy! Furthermore, we want to share it with those who don't know the truth about Christ Jesus! Do not be deceived, Nothing in this world will suffice (be enough)! In Jesus' mighty name, may the Holy Spirit of Truth, continue to bless us all; as we convey the message of Hope, from the wage of sin, through Faith in Christ Jesus!

August 7

Heavenly Father, We thank you for your word, which is alive in us! Your word came into the world from Heaven, to guide us all from the darkness of sin! Jesus is the word of God; and is one with the Father! May we become one with Jesus, so we can become one with the Father! In your word God, you guide us to the light! Your word is truth and there is no lie in thee! In Jesus' mighty name, Help us to stand for your word and not be deceived by man's lie!

August 2

As we embrace the Grace of God, that leads to salvation; a new creation emerges within us, from faith in Christ Jesus! No longer do we search the world for love and peace; instead we emulate the Prince of Peace, who is love! This transformation that takes place from Grace, continues by staying in Gods word! We overcome the difficulties of this world with Christ Jesus; and our fortitude comes from Him, who strengthens us! In Jesus' mighty name, May we all internalize the word of God, through faith in Christ Jesus!

August 3

The joy of the Lord, fills my heart completely! I lack nothing in Christ Jesus, because He loves me! My focus in life has drastically changed! I look to fill my days with virtue and not folly; Peace and not chaos; Love and not hate; Forgiveness and not resentment; Understanding, caring and concern for those suffering on their own accord! I want to introduce them to the Prince of Peace, whose love surpasses all understanding; and will suffice, for their tormenting pain! May the Grace of the Lord, that comes from God through faith in Christ Jesus, rest upon you all! In Jesus' mighty name!

August 4

May we as disciples of Christ Jesus, carry the love of God to every person we have contact with! May the harmony of love, be projected like a gentle Symphony of peace! May we convey the truth of Christ Jesus, in a way that attracts the doubters from all walks of life! May our tenacity to bring the truth of Christ Jesus, Prevail over the audacity and contempt from the doubters! Light Conquers Darkness and the love of Christ, Conquers all hate in the world! In Jesus' mighty name, may we be the presence of love to all the broken Hearted!

August 5

As we emulate the light of Christ Jesus, we become a guiding light to all those who are a slave to darkness (sin)! The love of Christ Jesus is light; and all those who embrace it are liberated from hatred and evil! Love is the greatest virtue; and Christ Jesus is love! As we become one with the Son of God, we become one with love! Love gives freely; and always receives more than it gives! The paradoxical reward of love, is that we never had so much love, until we shared it all with another! In Jesus' mighty name, let's emulate the love of God today!

August 6

The Salvation through faith in Christ Jesus, is what my spirit longs for, with great hope! I am but a mere example of the power of God, through faith in Christ Jesus! I wear the garment of righteousness, through the Son of God! Of myself, I wear the rags of sin! I am too blind to see, on my own accord! All that is good in me, comes from the one who saved me! Christ Jesus is He; the Prince of Peace! So don't remember me; for I am nothing without my Lord and Savior! I surrender all the temptations of sin at the foot of the cross; in the mighty name of Jesus, the Christ! I embrace the truth of Grace, through Christ Jesus with great joy; and it has become my breath of life, forevermore! May the peace beyond all understanding, rest upon us all who believe in Christ Jesus!

August 7

As we begin the day with the Lord, may we surrender all our selfish motives for glory and any self seeking gain! Let our mentality be altruistic (selfless) as we focus on others and their well being! Jesus, the Christ, came to serve and not be served! As we emulate His humility and love, we become true disciples of the Son of God! In Jesus' mighty name, may our characters speak louder than words as we express acts of kindness to all!

August 8

Being sure of the things we hope for, is trust; and that trust, that believes, is faith! Jesus is the truth that sets us free; from every negative thought that comes from me and the opinions from others; as well as the things that occur in this life! Find refuge (shelter) in Jesus; and be one with God, through faith in His Son! Stop doubting the truth of Christ Jesus; and embrace the Grace of love and mercy, that sets us all free; from this sinful world of lies! Trust the truth of Christ Jesus; and know a new freedom, that continues to keep us liberated, in all situations! May the truth of Christ Jesus, set us all free, in His Holy name!

August 9

Jesus is all we need; and He can provide all things through faith in Him! The mighty name of Jesus is more powerful than death; and His name will live forever! We proclaim life with Jesus over death, from the wage of sin! We bind all that is evil in the mighty name of Jesus; and by His authority, we are set free from all addictions, impulsive and compulsive behaviors, obsessions of the mind and all defects of character that interfere with the will of God! We claim victory over sin, in the mighty name of Jesus!

August 10

May the light of the Lord, guide us all, in times of darkness! As we internalize the word of God through Faith in Christ Jesus, the birth of salvation begins! As we move away from sinful behavior and allow the word of God to guide us, we become one with God! As we become one with God, we become servants to all! In Jesus' mighty name, may we all utilize the word of God, to guide others from the lie of the world!

Things to strive for:
    Resist what is evil, and dance with virtue, to the rhythm of love! Ignore negativity, and become the hope, that kindness instills! Be impatient about nothing; but in all ways show the peaceful restraint of a gentle person!

August 11

Heavenly Father, We come to you with a grateful heart, for all that you did and do for us! Your word is alive in our character! We turn away from sin, like a hand from a hot flame! We speak in a skillful way, to bring GLORY to your name! We hunger for righteousness, through faith in your Son Jesus! What we can't do alone, you make possible with faith! In Jesus' mighty name, Help us all to project your love in every situation!

August 12

As I travel closer to the truth, I see how lost I was in the lie! My honesty is contingent on revealing the lie that I denied for so long! The truth of God, has brought light into the darkness in my life! Many belief systems I defended and protected turned out to be erroneous to the truth of Christ Jesus! Now that I can see where I've been blind, the changes to be in compliance with the will of God can happen! I must surrender all, so I can begin to receive! May the truth of Christ Jesus, set me free from the lies in the world; and the lies in me! In the mighty name of Jesus, I pray for all of us!

August 13

How great thou art, no one can fathom! For you created all things, for your Glory! You came down from Heaven, to guide the lost back to you through faith in the Son of God! God, you are the beginning and the end! Through faith in your Son Jesus, we are saved from our iniquity! For you and your Son are one! As we take Jesus the Christ into our hearts, we take you Father God, into our hearts! In Jesus' mighty name, may we all take the Son of God into our hearts, to know the Father!

August 14

Born again by faith in Christ Jesus; the Son of God our Father! A new creation spawned by love! No fault will be used against thy children of faith! All Glory to you Father God; the Creator of every good thing! May I bring Glory to your name, by expressing love to the lost; and leading many by the name of Yeshua/Jesus! In Jesus' mighty name, help us all to be obedient children of the most High God!

From Fear to Faith:

Fear tried to talk, but faith interrupted; Negative projection of painful destruction! New in the faith and under construction; willing to be guided, and take heed to instructions! Now I have peace through Christ, with no interruptions!

August 15

Lord Jesus, your message is hope; from all trials, tribulations and tragedies! Through faith in you, we are free from the bondage of sin! Help us all by the power of the Holy Spirit, to lead the lost to you! Guide us with your light of love and understanding! In Jesus' mighty name, may the wisdom of God be spoken to all those poor in spirit; and may the encouragement of your love, heal all that is broken in the doubters; and guide them back to you!

August 16

For those motivated and encapsulated by greed and admiration, looking for validation from the lost; nothing accomplished will suffice! Searching endlessly in the lie, will bring no truth! Until all that was pursued comes to a halt, no fulfillment will be felt! Surrendering self for others, is the great gain in life; as peaceful liberation is born from death to self! In Jesus' mighty name!

A daily mantra:
Look to succeed to feed the poor; not to feed our greed for more!

August 17

As we follow the Lords directions of perfection through faith in Him; we know a new peace! Of ourselves, we lack much; but in Christ Jesus, we don't lack anything! Our hope grows daily, as we internalize the words of God; through the Messiah! Jesus is He! We see past the short term struggles in this life, and look forward to the peace to come in the next! In Jesus' mighty name, may we all utilize the words of God, to serve others in their time of need!

August 18

The love of the Lord sets me free, from the hate in the world and the negativity in me! For where there is love, all good dwells! As I meditate on the love of Christ Jesus, I become one with love! I replace darkness with light and refuse to go back to my sinful ways! I rejoice in the serene freedom of love, that keeps me yoked to the most High God, through our Lord Jesus, the Christ! May our character be the expression of love to all! To be one with love, is to be one with God! In Jesus' loving name!

August 19

May not one thought take me away from your righteousness Lord! Whatever blocks your will in me to serve others, remove it from me, in Jesus' mighty name! I know I am weak on my own accord; and that I fall short of the glory of God! It's through faith in you Jesus, that all things good become possible! I surrender all of me, for your love Lord! The love that doesn't run out and isn't contingent on what I can do right; but is contingent on faith in you, as the Son of the living God! I Believe in you Jesus; and you are my Savior!

August 20

Heavenly Father, I come to you and ask that you guide me today with the Holy Spirit of Truth; that comes upon me from Faith in your Son Jesus! Help me to see the part I play in any chaos in my life or the lives of others! Help me, to not force my will upon anybody; but in all ways to emulate the love of Christ Jesus; and be a servant to all! May I serve all your children with love, peace, generosity, humility, and hope from the Grace of God, through faith in Christ Jesus! In the mighty name of Jesus, I ask for your help in my life, to do your will!

August 21

May the habitual thoughts of negativity be overcome By the Holy Spirit of truth; in Jesus' mighty name! May the vulgarity of emotions, be overcome by the loving virtue of patience! May the light of God, shine through me today, by emulating the love of Christ Jesus! May my acts of kindness, through showing deep compassion for those who suffer, turn foes, into faithful friends! In the most Holy name of Jesus, I pray for all those hurting today!

August 22

We need the discernment from God, to know our purpose; and we need wise counsel, to grow to our potential. The good news is, we get both from Christ Jesus and much more! We can also have the courage to ask for help, from those that have been where we are, and found a way out. We can duplicate the success of our predecessors; instead of complicating the growth God has in store for us! May the truth of Christ Jesus, set you free from the lie in the world! May the peace and love of the Lord, bless us all! In Jesus' mighty name, we pray!

August 23

May the loving sacrifice of Christ Jesus be upon you and all those you hold dear! May the love that conquers all hate be the focus of your mind! May compassion move you into action; to serve in an altruistic way! May you be excessively preoccupied to love and express love all day long; without hidden motives! May the peace and freedom that comes from Christ Jesus, and his unconditional love, be upon all who desire the truth of God! In Jesus' loving name, we pray!

August 24

As we feed on the bread of life, which is Christ Jesus; the truth lives in us, and no sin of lies can reside! As we drink the blood of Jesus, which was shed for all; we become one with God, through the Son; and we sacrifice ourselves for others, in an altruistic (selfless) way! We no longer belong to the world! We now belong to the Father, through faith in His Son! Now we can be in the house of the Lord forever, which is Heaven; through the blood and body of Christ! In Jesus' mighty name!

August 25

Our compassion that comes from the Lord, goes into the suffering with light and love! We are guides, entrusted by God, through faith in His Son Jesus! We guide the lost with love and respect! We speak words of life, into the wage of sin; and guide the doubter by the words of God, through Faith in Christ Jesus! We are the church! We guide by the power of the Holy Spirit of Truth! That truth is Jesus! He is the only way to salvation! In Jesus' mighty name, may we allow God to lead us, as we guide others, to take Christ Jesus, into their hearts!

August 26

May the love of Christ Jesus bless you, when you share yourself, as one filled with love! May we give to others, as God has given to us! May the gift of giving suffice! May we strive to serve others and not ourselves! May we experience the fullness of love that manifests through service to all! May we share the truth of Christ Jesus, as the greatest gift given to inherit reconciliation with God! Blessings to all that choose to believe in Christ Jesus! May we guide the doubter with love as our example!

August 27

Be not afraid! Replace your fear with faith! Fear is the negative projection of what might happen when your self talk is dominating you! Hope is the positive projection of Christ Jesus, being in our future, before we arrive! Put all your hope in God; and not in your own understanding or lack of! See what you can do for another and free yourself from self centered fear! May the peace of the Lord, rest upon all those who seek Him; in Jesus' mighty name!

August 28

Regardless of the circumstances in these times, or times of old, with Christ Jesus, there is always hope! Lean not on your own understanding; and don't let the lack of understanding overwhelm you! With faith, all things are possible; and they can be overcome with peace! As disciples of Christ Jesus, we carry a message of hope; and a promise of freedom; from the wage of sin; through Faith in the Messiah! Christ Jesus is He! The Son of God! Don't worry yourselves about the flesh; when only faith in Christ Jesus, can save your soul! Embrace that truth, that conquers all fear! Be liberated, by the truth of Christ Jesus; and guide others, as the Church of Faith that lives in the hearts of all believers!

August 29

When we trust the Lord with all our heart, mind and soul, peace becomes our shadow! Putting all our trust in God, will never disappoint us! There is comfort in knowing Christ Jesus! As we understand you more, we become less; and follow the light that brings peace into suffering! God, you are the most compassionate! Your love takes away all suffering! Our refuge is in you and you alone, through faith in your Son Jesus! As we abide in you, our folly dissipates! How we yearn for your righteousness, as your word guides us correctly! All glory belongs to God and not ourselves! For anything good that comes from us, was created by you!

August 30

Christ Jesus is truth and no lie can stand against Him! Where we are weak, Christ Jesus is strong! His strength is increased through our faith! The eyes of faith, see Christ Jesus coming into the darkness of our lives; and bringing the light of hope! No hope in the Lord is done in vain! See past the difficulties in this life with great joy; and may your hope in the Lord, help you to persevere! In Jesus' mighty name!

August 31

As we emulate the love of Christ Jesus, peace becomes our shadow and kindness becomes our light! All that's good in the spirit, becomes our motives! Our aspirations are altruistic (selfless) in thought and in deed! We look to guide others to the truth of Christ Jesus, for their salvation! We give all Glory to God, who enlightens us all, through faith in Christ Jesus and by the power of the Holy Spirit! In Jesus' mighty name, may we all see the truth in the Son of God; and look to emulate His love forever!

September 1

How shall I express the love I have for you, Lord? There are not enough words that would suffice, in the expression of love for you, God! There's nothing I can do, that would come close to the Holy Sacrifice of your Son Jesus! Your love God, knows no bounds! It's astounding to all things created! To know your love, is a peaceful tranquility, that gives birth to the hope of salvation! A priceless gift, from excruciating love! How can I not endure all things through you, when you endured all things for us; for the forgiveness of our sins! You are my strength, my light and my great joy! Lord God, you fill me up completely with your love! ILOVEU God, with all my heart, soul, mind and strength! In the mighty name of Jesus, may I express this love to all your children!

September 2

Lord God, we thank you for these difficult times, so that we can draw closer to you in faith! As we endure all things, through faith in you Jesus, we grow in character to serve those you have chosen! Our thoughts are on your promise, which gives birth to our hope! We see past all struggles, with great joy in our hearts, through faith in Christ Jesus! In Jesus' mighty name, help us to guide others to you!

September 3

Lord God, you are the Vine and we are your branches; through faith in your Son Jesus! Help us to convey the message of hope, to the hopeless! May the Holy Spirit of Truth, guide every word from our lips! May the doubter turn away from their erroneous beliefs and embrace the Grace of God, through Christ Jesus! May our character emulate the light and love of the Lord! May all those who feel lost and alone be filled with the Holy Spirit, through Faith in Christ Jesus! In Jesus' mighty name, we pray!

September 4

I must profess, that without Christ Jesus as my Lord and Savior, I am nothing! You Lord are the light in my darkness! The truth to every lie in the world and in my thoughts! As I aspire to be more like you and die to self; peace becomes my shadow from your light! Although I was not present when you walked among us, I see you in everything! Your word is alive in me and in many of my brothers and sisters of faith! We know you are the Messiah! The Son of God! The Lamb of God, who takes away the sins of the world! May we reject every form of sin, by the power of the Holy Spirit, in Jesus' mighty name!

September 5

Today, let's meditate on every word of God, through faith in Christ Jesus! Let us reflect on all the Lord has endured, so we could be forgiven! As we internalize the word of God, we see the error in our ways! We ask in the mighty name of Jesus, to cleanse us, of all unrighteousness! May we resist all temptations, by the power of the Holy Spirit! In Jesus' Holy name, we pray!

September 6

The wage of sin is death! Yet, Jesus has risen and beat death! Let's all embrace the truth of Christ Jesus and repent from our sins! Jesus made salvation possible through faith in Him! Blessed are those who Believe without seeing! May the Holy Spirit of Truth, guide us all from the lie of this world! In Jesus' mighty name, let's celebrate the good news of Christ Jesus with all!

September 7

The Lord has mercy, on the sinner who seeks Him! He gives Grace, to the one who repents with faith in Him! Christ Jesus, is the Lord of Lords! In His light, there is no darkness! In His truth, there is no lie! Accept this gift of salvation and turn away from every sin! Do not entertain any form of sin and embrace the love of the Lord extended to all! In Jesus' mighty name!

The rewards of knowing Yeshua:
    To know Jesus, is to know hope! To believe in Jesus, is to be set free from all fear! To abide in the Lord, is to live in truth! To find refuge in Christ Jesus, is to be kept safe from insidious foes! To love Jesus, is to never hate again! To have faith in Yeshua/Jesus, is to live forever in Paradise/Heaven!

September 8

Our relationship with the Lord, enables us to turn chaos into clarity; and pain into growth, through persevering! Being in the yoke with Christ Jesus, turns our weaknesses into strengths; as we learn from the Son of God! Allowing the Holy Spirit of Truth to guide us, turns ignorance into wisdom! Our progress in difficulties, comes from faith in the Lord; who uses all things, for His good purpose! We are called to serve others, as we would do for ourselves! The love of God, dominates all negativity! God's light is found in Christ Jesus! In Jesus' mighty name, may all who struggle, embrace the truth of Christ Jesus and be released from all torment!

September 9

Traditions, do not Trump truth! Christ Jesus, is TRUTH! If you are not standing up for the truth of Christ Jesus, then you are falling for the lie of this world! If you formed an opinion with contempt for Jesus, you don't understand the Holy Sacrifice given to the world with the greatest love! If your faith derives from your father and his traditions or someone else's which is not of Christ, it is erroneous to the truth of God; and its all for naught! Faith in Christ Jesus is a must, not an option! He is the only way to the Father! Moreover, He is the only truth that matters in this world and the next! Take the Son of God into your heart and make Jesus your Lord and Savior! Move away from your sins by the power of the Holy Spirit and emulate the love of Christ to all, in Jesus' mighty name!

September 10

It's by faith in Christ Jesus that I've died to all self seeking and selfish ambitions! Now with true humility, I put others before myself to serve! I serve in truth, with the love of the Lord; and I am patient with the doubter! I rejoice in faith, with all my brothers and sisters in Christ! The illusion of this world doesn't deceive us of the true Vine! We see it as a blocker to all doubters! We surrender all things that interfere with the Gospel; and our characters are one with the Lord of peace! We speak with kindness, compassion and the love that shares the good news with the lost! We are single minded in the Lord of Lords! In the mighty name of Jesus, may we not lose one for your kingdom who is willing to know you!

September 11

It's through faith in Christ Jesus that we have a promise to be reconciled with God! Our Hope is in this promise and the gift is immediate peace, through the Holy Spirit of truth! We ask God the Father, through His Son, and in union with the Holy Spirit of truth, to guide us, to guide others to the truth of Christ Jesus; and the hope that brings peace beyond all understanding! May our hope in the Lord, eliminate all anxiety! May our faith in Christ Jesus conquer all negativity, in this world and in our minds! In Jesus' mighty name, we pray!

September 12

As I put on the yoke to be one with Christ Jesus; I abide in His love that is one with God! This makes accepting the difficulties in this life easier and the ability to have peace! I don't allow the world to dictate my attitude; for my trust in the Lord helps me overcome all negativity! I am filled with the love that doesn't run out; and I share this love with all! May the peace that comes from the never ending love of Christ, be upon you all; in the mighty name of Jesus!

September 13

As children of the most high God, through faith in Christ Jesus, we have a responsibility to the doubters; by helping them see the love of the Lord! We do this by being compassionate, and remaining steadfast in our faith in Christ Jesus; as well as being generous and understanding! We guide with the light of the Lord working through us; as we internalize and utilize the word of God to guide others! In Jesus' mighty name, may we be open to receiving the Holy Spirit of truth; so we are not blind guides!

September 14

As we die to self daily, the truth of Christ Jesus comes into His new creation, through our faithful obedience! We are new creations through faith and no record of wrongs, is brought forth pertaining to us in Christ! If in ourselves we lack much in union with Christ Jesus we don't lack anything! For where we are weak, His strength is perfected! We lean not on our own understanding, but on every word that proceedeth out of the mouth of God! For the Father and the Son are one light that is love! All knowing Father God, we submit to you in the mighty name of Jesus and by the power of your Holy Spirit! Guide us in all your ways!

September 15

God the Father, who gave us His Son; is all loving, all knowing and completely powerful! All GLORY and honor belongs to thee! May our faith in Christ Jesus please thee! For in all things, we fall short of the glory of God! Your word is truth; as the Son of man is truth! As we take the Messiah into our hearts, your word becomes alive in us! For the word of God and the Son are one! May the Holy Spirit of Truth, guide us all in faith, as we surrender completely to you! In Jesus' mighty name, we pray!

September 16

Lord God, you are the Truth; and no one can know the truth without you! Christ Jesus, is the way to the truth; and He is one with the Father! Anyone who doesn't know Jesus in their hearts and doesn't believe He is the Messiah, doesn't know the truth; for Jesus is the Truth, and the only way to the Father! The only truth I know, is Jesus; and of myself, I am nothing without Him! Your word God, is Truth! In that word, is your Son! In Jesus' mighty name, may the Truth of your word, through faith in your Son, be alive in us all!

September 17

Jesus is the breath of life for all eternity! May we put all our hope in Him and trust that it will produce ever lasting peace that comes from His love! Nothing in this world is more important than our faith in Christ Jesus! We were created for God's Glory and not our own! Embrace the truth of Jesus and stop listening to the lie of the doubter! May you accept the truth of Christ Jesus and allow that truth to set you free!

September 18

In the yoke with Christ Jesus we learn from the master of the universe! He is one with the Father who helped create all things! How easy it is to trust thee! You have saved us from our iniquity! Our sinful ways, are not your ways; and we look to emulate your loving Grace to all! As you walk beside us in this yoke of Holiness, may we learn compassion from thee; to go into the suffering and guide others out with the same gentle love that was given to us, from you! There is rest for our souls in the yoke with Jesus! In Jesus' mighty name, let's guide others to Jesus; by showing great compassion, to those in need!

September 19

To count my sins would be endless; but through faith in Christ Jesus my sins are no longer counted against me; and I'm forgiven! Now I can put on the garment of righteousness, through faith in the Son of God; of myself, I fall short of this glory! In me, there is nothing righteous! It's faith in the Messiah that sets me apart; no works from myself are counted as righteous! All Glory belongs to God the Father; through faith in His only begotten Son! In Jesus' mighty name, let's share the good news of Salvation with all that are willing to receive it!

September 20

As children of the most High God, through faith in Christ Jesus, we are to emulate His love and be guided by His teachings! We should be quick to forgive all wrong doings, as we have been forgiven through faith in Christ Jesus (Grace)! We are to be one with love, that is made of many virtues; working for the good of one another in Christ our Lord! May the peace that comes from love, emanate from our spirits! May we stand for the truth of Christ Jesus and not fall for the hate in this world! May the peace of the Lord, conquer all negativity in your life!

September 21

May our beliefs that are not in compliance with the will of God, through Christ Jesus, be surrendered! May we be obedient children of God, through Faith in His Holy Son Jesus! May our focus be virtuous and not vice or malice! May we yearn for righteousness through the word of God, spoken through His Son, the Messiah! May we become the peace and love we seek, through Christ Jesus; and by the power of the Holy Spirit! In Jesus' mighty name, we pray!

September 22

It is our faith in Christ Jesus that conquers sin; of ourselves, we are all sinful and fall short of the Glory of God! Jesus, the Christ, intercedes on our behalf, through faith in Him and not by works; so no one can boast! In Jesus' mighty name, may we surrender all doubt to God, through faith in Christ Jesus!

Holy Surrender Prayer

Lord Jesus, I come to you completely surrendered in your Holy Name! Remove all my desires and concerns that block your truth and my relationship with you! Guide me by the power of the Holy Spirit, to speak your wisdom and share your love with all believers and non-believers! In Jesus' mighty name, I pray!

September 23

The word of God, through His Son Jesus, is a melody for my soul! The dance is love; and it is a selfless dance! It is performed with humility; as we allow difficult circumstances to motivate faith with works! We become active with compassion for the less fortunate! This rhythm of love is contagious to the hearts and souls of the doubters and believers alike! In Jesus' loving name, may the word of God be alive in you; as a symphony that moves one's soul!

September 24

The thoughts of sinful behavior is repulsive to a disciple of Christ Jesus! To act contrary to the truth of Jesus, is tormenting to the one who persists in sin! Once we submit to the truth of Christ Jesus, we become sanctified in the spirit! When sanctification takes hold of us, we are born again in spirit! Moreover, we no longer live by the flesh, but are lead by the Holy Spirit! In Jesus' mighty name, may we who believe in Christ, emulate the truth of Jesus!

September 25

May we not live in the sin, but in the lesson; It's through faith in Christ Jesus that we know the blessing! Your words Lord, are a guiding light to all lost in the darkness of sin! The torment of sin is crushed by your unending love! It's through faith in Christ Jesus, that we know Salvation; and no one can boast about it; for it is the greatest gift given, through faith and not works! In Jesus' mighty name, may we share this gift with a character filled with love and words of hope!

September 26

To know the truth of Christ Jesus and to go back to the lie of sin, is to know torment! We are called to be examples of Christ; by expressing the message of Grace to all nations in a gentle way! We are to project love to those who earned it and those who didn't! We are becoming the love of Christ Jesus, as we die to self daily! Our motives are pure and authentic connections of love that are conveyed by selfless acts of kindness, compassion and generosity! May the doubter want to know more; by the love of Jesus, that we express in our character! In Jesus' mighty name, let us be the love of the Lord to all!

September 27

My hope is in the Lord alone! Nothing in this world will suffice (be enough)! You heard my cry and rescued me! I was lost and you corrected the error in my ways! Christ Jesus, you are in my future before I arrive! Salvation is in you alone! May my ways be in compliance with your will! In Jesus' mighty name, I surrender my life to God in every way; and may your love become greater in me every day!

September 28

The best way we can invite others to know Jesus, the Christ, is by projecting the love of God unconditionally! For God is love! Furthermore, God and Jesus are one! The love we project, through Faith in Christ, keeps us in union with the Father and the Son! We become the love we seek when we take Christ Jesus into our hearts! That's the love that drives out all fear and dominates all darkness! It is the light of the Lord that comforts the lost; with a direction towards perfection, in Jesus' mighty name!

September 29

Through the surrender of self to God, through faith in Christ Jesus, I have come to the end of self-centeredness and to the beginning of God consciousness! I have never had so much love, until I have become the principles of love, through emulating Christ Jesus! As I strive to serve and not be served, I become the altruistic love that is one with God and the universe! Therefore, my self-love is no longer about self and what I can accomplish; but what I can give away with love to help others! In conclusion to a topic that never ends, but can always become more, I say this; that we never had so much, until we gave it all away with love!

September 30

Our Father God (Yahweh), has sent His Son Jesus (Yeshua) into the world; to guide us from our sinful nature, so we can have reconciliation with the Father, through Faith in His Son! For all those who reject this truth, they reject God! How can anyone mistreat a child and expect to be in good standing with that child's father! So how can anyone pray to the Father and not accept the Messiah Jesus, as the Son of the most High God of light? In the decision of not accepting the Son of light, they choose to stay in darkness forever! May everyone reading this, repent from their sins and accept Jesus into their hearts, so their sins may be forgiven; and they may receive eternal life! In the mighty name of Jesus, I pray for all God's children!

October 1

If we learn from the world and it is not the truth of God, then we have many issues and beliefs that are erroneous! We must get honest by checking our motives; and seeing the part we play in the lie! As we open ourselves up to the truth of Christ Jesus, He guides us from darkness to light! From lies to truth! From chaos to clarity! From insanity to tranquility! From evil to love! May we embrace the truth of Christ Jesus and may that truth set us free from all iniquity! In the mighty name of Jesus, we all Pray!

October 2

We believe everything Christ Jesus said! If Jesus said it, that settles it! We follow all His teachings to the best of our ability! Jesus never said worship a God of your own understanding! Furthermore, Jesus never said you can believe in me if you want! Jesus did say, I am the way, the truth and the life; No one comes to the Father except through me! Faith in Jesus allows God's mercy to come into fruition! Salvation is only possible through faith in Christ Jesus! That's our belief 100%! May the Good Lord show you this truth! In Jesus' mighty name, we pray!

October 3

For all that are hungry and thirsty for peace and love, they will be satisfied, by taking Jesus into their hearts; and following His words! Faith in Christ Jesus, will suffice for all struggles in this life! He is the way, when we lose our way! As we center ourselves through prayer with Jesus; the Holy Spirit will enlighten us! God sees and hears all things! Trust in the Lord thy God, through Christ Jesus! May that which is hidden, be revealed to all that have faith in Christ Jesus!

October 4

As the Lord is one with the truth; let us be one with the Lord! We as disciples of Christ Jesus, submit in every way to the truth of God! We surrender our old ways and become new creations through faith in Christ Jesus! We live by virtue to serve one another with love! As we come to know love, we become intimate with our Lord and Savior, Jesus the Christ! We put others before ourselves, with authentic humility! The love of the Lord speaks through our compassion for one another! In Jesus' mighty name, may we emulate the love that is truth!

October 5

As we eat the bread of life and digest the word of God through Christ Jesus, we become one with God! As we drink the blood of Christ Jesus, we become one with the resurrection and eternal life! With a new hope in the life to come and the love of the Lord in our hearts, we share the good news with all who are willing to hear it and receive it! May the power of the Holy Spirit, be upon all who look to share the good news (Gospel) of Christ Jesus! In Jesus' mighty name, we pray!

October 6

To project the love of the Lord is our goal for each day! Without love, success is not possible! For what does a person gain without love? Little in life, becomes much with love; as much means little, without love! Jesus the Christ, showed us through many examples, on how we should be the love we seek in this life! He shared with the doubter that faith in Him, is the way to the Father! He healed the sick, fed the hungry, gave to the poor in spirit, raised the dead and much more! He took nothing; and gave everything; including His life for the forgiveness of our sins; not His; for He was without sin! When we emulate the love of Christ Jesus, we give, instead of take; and the success of love becomes our shadow, from the Lords loving light! We realize the paradoxical reward of love; which is we never had so much love, until we gave it all away! Now the success of love doesn't elude our spirit; as we stop looking to fulfill the desires of our flesh!

October 7

The temptations of this world are many for the one who lives on their own accord! For the one who is sanctified in the spirit, the flesh is not entertained! The word of God, through Christ Jesus, is truth; in that truth, we abide! As we remain open to receive the truth, we surrender the temptations of this world to Christ Jesus! As we internalize the word of God, through faith in His Son; we utilize His truth, by the power of the Holy Spirit, to guide others, from the temptations of sin! In Jesus' mighty name, may we all stay sanctified in the spirit, so we don't fall for the sins of this world!

October 8

Heavenly Father God, in the name of Jesus Your Son, I surrender myself to You completely!

May I put the least among us, before myself; as I serve them with acts of kindness!

May I show the peaceful restraint, of a flexible servant of the most High God!

May the negative reactions of others, build my character with love!

May I set healthy boundaries, that can speak up, without putting other people down!

May I make the day about altruistic acts and eliminate self seeking motives in all its forms!

In the precious name of Jesus the Christ, I pray!

October 9

The love for the Lord grows in us, with every act of kindness for one another! We guide others with the love of Christ Jesus in our character! Give no reason to dissuade the doubter, from faith in the Son of God! Jesus is He! As we emulate the love of the Lord, by serving all; we persuade the unbelievers through our actions and our character! In Christ Jesus' mighty name, may the Holy Spirit of Truth, guide us in every way; so that we don't lose one doubter to the kingdom of God!

October 10

No one is the truth of God, except Christ Jesus! May the Holy Spirit of Truth, guide us all that are willing to be obedient to the word of God; through faith in Jesus the Christ! May we speak words of faith into the doubters life! May we as faithful servants of the Lord, surrender everything mental, physical and spiritual that is not the will of God! May we not fluctuate in faith to accommodate the doubters of Christ Jesus! May we stand steadfast, with the Son of God! In Jesus' mighty name, may the word of God, lead us all in guiding others to the Messiah!

October 11

Don't let other people's actions, dictate an overreaction from you! May the negative actions of others, propel a peaceful restraint from you! May you weigh your options on how to handle the situation in an assertive way. Remember, the more difficult the situation, the more growth in your character you will have as you persevere through the difficult trials! In Jesus' mighty name, may we all get our strength from the Lord to persevere!

October 12

As we start this day, may we be open to all that is good in Christ Jesus! May we put those in need, before any greed! May we yearn for truth, through the word of God; Christ Jesus is the word! May we stand steadfast (unwavering) in the faith of Yeshua/Jesus; even in the presence of the unbeliever with contempt! May we hunger for righteousness, through the examples of our Lord Jesus! In Jesus' powerful name, we surrender anything that is not the will of God; with contrite spirits!

October 13

May we not live in the sin, but in the lesson; It's through faith in Christ Jesus, that we know the blessing! Your words Lord, are a guiding light; to all lost in the darkness of sin! The torment of sin, is crushed by your unending love! It's through faith in you Christ Jesus, that we know salvation; no one can boast about it, for it is the greatest gift given, through faith and not by works! In Jesus' mighty name, may we share this gift with a character of love and words of hope!

October 14

Heavenly Father,

Fill us with the Holy Spirit of Truth, in Jesus' mighty name! May we be filled with your love, so we search no more! May we share your love with all; so all know you, through us! Your truth is love, and it saves all, from the lie in the world! There is no fear in your love! Your love is light and it eliminates all darkness! May the positive projection of your love, be our goal for this day! May it be freely given; as you freely give! In Jesus' mighty name, let's all emulate the love of God today!

October 15

To really understand the magnitude of God giving us Jesus, to be crucified for the forgiveness of sins; is beyond our human understanding! The pain of this great gift to God, cannot be fathomed! Everything the Son of God experienced, God the Father felt! This precious gift from God and the obedience of Christ Jesus, is something I embrace with all my heart, soul, mind and strength! Everyone is welcomed to receive this gift from God, through Faith in Jesus; His only begotten Son! Don't reject this gift that was the ultimate price paid for our Salvation! Today, I receive Jesus Christ as my Lord and Savior! Where we are weak, be our strength Lord! Our Hope is in you alone! This hope helps us to persevere with courage and strength! May we live to serve the least among us; in Jesus' mighty name!

October 16

As we guide others by the power of the Holy Spirit, we are to conform to the word of God; through faith in Christ Jesus! We are a vessel of love, guided by the light of Jesus, as our rudder in our journey! We are held more accountable than others, because we guide God's children! We must practice what we preach and teach to all that are willing to follow! Our meekness is to the word of God and not to the ways of the world! In Jesus' mighty name, may we be willing to die daily to all self seeking motives!

October 17

Jesus is the way, for all of us who lost our way! Jesus is the truth that sets us free; from all the lies inside our mind; and in the world! The wage of sin, that cost all doubters everlasting life; has been conquered, by Jesus' precious blood! Faith in Christ Jesus is the admission to be reconciled with God the FATHER! Today I pray, that we all have the kind of faith in Christ Jesus, that doesn't bargain or negotiate with any form of sin; but chooses Holy Surrender to the way, the truth, and the life, in Jesus' mighty name!

October 18

It is God who makes all things possible; therefore, I surrender my pride! It's faith in Christ Jesus, that saves my soul; therefore, I cannot boast! It's by the word of God, that wisdom comes into fruition; therefore, I surrender my own understanding! It is by loving others, without hidden motives, that I become one with God; therefore, I surrender all self-centeredness! It is by sharing, all that I have been given by God, to know fulfillment; therefore, I surrender all covetousness (desire for something another possesses)! In the Holy name of Jesus, may we all die to self daily!

October 19

May the difficulties of the day, motivate you to seek the most High God, through faith in Christ Jesus! May perseverance that comes from faith in the Son of God, strengthen you where you are weak! May your character bring hope to the suffering individuals that you come in contact with! May they know the love of God, through your acts of kindness; and faith in Christ Jesus! With authentic humility, may Jesus the Christ, bless all of you, before me!

October 20

We have Grace by Faith in Christ Jesus and not by works; so no one can boast! It's a gift from God! That does not give us a pass to continue to sin and try to manipulate this great gift from God! We may fall short on many levels; but we aspire to live by virtue, and not by vice! As we die to self daily; we are living to serve the Lord, and not every sinful desire! May we lead by example, so the doubters will be intrigued to know more! May our character let everyone know, that we are followers of Christ Jesus; our Lord and Savior! Let's be a blessing, from the many lessons of God's word, through faith in His Son Jesus!

October 21

The wage of sin is death; but having Faith in Christ Jesus has conquered death! Our human nature is weak; but the Son of God is strong! We don't lean on our own understanding according to the law; for we fall short on our own accord! It's only through Faith in Christ Jesus, that we can be saved from our sinful nature! We aspire to live by love in all it's forms and die to self seeking motives daily! May Jesus become more in us, as we become less; so we can serve many, in Jesus' mighty name!

October 22

As we abide in Christ Jesus, He abides in us! The word of God is alive in us and we feel compelled to share the good news with everyone! For we are with the truth of Christ Jesus! We look to serve and not be served! We love, because He first loved us! We walk in righteousness through faith in Christ Jesus! On our own understanding, we are lost! We lean on the word of God, through Christ Jesus; and He prevents us from falling for the ways of the world! In Jesus' mighty name, may the word of God be our refuge!

October 23

When we surrender ourselves to Jesus, we surrender all pride! We no longer look to bring glory to our name; but to the one who saved us from eternal damnation! Great things begin to occur when we surrender completely! We no longer make the day and all its activities about us! We become free from self and the opinions of others! We put the least among us, before us, in true humility! Virtue, becomes achievable through authentic love, for our fellow man, woman and child; the latter being first! We don't take insults personally, we detach in loving prayer! We become the peace we seek, through the Holy Spirit of truth, in Jesus' mighty name!

October 24

Lord, you are my hope in every situation; you are my light in every dark time! My faith in you, is rewarded with Salvation! I move away from evil, with great joy for thee! I sing praises in your Holy Name; as I repent with tears of joy! Yeshua is the way, everyday! My heart sings words of love and adoration for the Son of God! Christ Jesus is He! Embrace this truth with all thy heart and repent from thy sins of old! Be obedient, as children of the most High God! Jesus is one with He! In Jesus' most Holy name, let's exalt His name forever!

October 25

It's through faith in Christ Jesus, that the hope of salvation becomes possible! As we repent from our sins, through faith in the Son of God; the Holy Spirit of truth becomes our guide! May we be quick to be patient and kind! May we be a friend, instead of looking for one! Our motives are authentic, and they bring glory to God and not ourselves! We are motivated by love and guided by the wisdom of God! In Jesus' mighty name, may we stay yoked to Jesus, as we serve all!

October 26

Embracing The Grace

Embracing the Grace, takes me to a new place... That puts a smile on my shameful face.... No more lies about who I am; Letting Jesus be my best friend.... I'm forgiven by God, through faith in His Son; Now the healing has begun! I forgive myself, and others too; because Jesus is forgiveness, all the way through! To not forgive, is a sin; that keeps hate alive, and no one wins!

By your loving servant

October 27

In the mighty name of Jesus, may we all be open to receive the truth of God! May we surrender anything that blocks God's blessings! May we internalize the word of God; which is Christ Jesus! May the truth of Christ Jesus, set us free from our sinful nature! May we utilize the commandments of the Messiah, to love one another completely! Heavenly Father, we surrender all of us to you; guide us in all your ways, through faith in your Son Jesus/Yeshua ! In Jesus' mighty name, we pray!

October 28

As we surrender all of ourselves to Christ Jesus, we feel true peace for the first time! As we serve others with no hidden motives, we feel completely satisfied! The more we give, the less we need! This is the paradoxical reward of love! Until we know God, through faith in Christ Jesus, love continues to be fleeting! In Jesus' mighty name, may we become the love we seek, through faith in Christ Jesus, so we search no more; then love won't elude us, but become our shadow, from the Lords Great light!

October 29

As followers of the truth through faith in Christ Jesus, we have an obligation to live by virtue! We guide by example, from a character that is above reproach! We speak words of life into the world by sharing the good news (Gospel) of Christ Jesus! In Jesus' mighty name, may we express love to the doubters so they are motivated to know Christ Jesus through our acts of kindness!

October 30

The Lord Christ Jesus is love; and whoever knows the love of the Lord, projects that love to his brothers and sisters! Be the love of the Lord and you will search no more, for that which you have become! As the Lord gives love, we must give love! When we put others before ourselves with love in our hearts, we emulate the love of Christ Jesus to all! True humility is conveyed in this way!

October 31

Our greatest accomplishments have to do with others!

To feed the hungry, with love and food; to greet strangers with a smile, although I was in a bad mood; to share the little I have, with the one who has none; to help the weak, get the job done; to be a friend to the lonely and the one with many foes; to be quick to forgive, and let all grudges go; to freely give, as Christ Jesus freely gave to me; to love with no strings, is for all to be free!

November 1

As we surrender all that is not Holy; we solidify the sanctification of our Lord and Savior Christ Jesus! For the Lord is Holy; and we are called to be Holy, through faith in the Lord! We live Holy by following the teachings of Christ Jesus! All that encompasses the love of God is Holy! In Jesus' mighty name, may we be open and willing to receive the Holy Spirit of Truth, to remain Holy, through faith in Christ Jesus!

November 2

Do not be deceived by anyone's sinful nature! Do not entertain debauchery in your mind; but surrender all difficulties to our Lord Jesus, the Christ; who has defeated sin and makes victory attainable through Faith in Him! Do not associate with those who enjoy sinning; but guide those who want a way out! Share the Gospel, and you share a solution through Faith in Christ Jesus! Be the light of the Lord, and darkness cannot over take you! May Jesus the Christ, be with us all, in Jesus' mighty name!

November 3

For those that doubt what they don't understand, faith in Christ Jesus is a far reach; for those that are not willing to receive or believe in the truth of God! We must not lean on our own understanding; but on every word that proceedeth out of the mouth of God, through Christ Jesus! For us who have faith in Christ Jesus, we know a new freedom that is conceived from an everlasting hope; that will not fail or fall short! I pray, in the mighty name of Jesus, that everyone who doubts or doesn't believe because they don't understand, embraces the truth of Jesus the Christ; and receives Salvation, from faith and not works!

November 4

Let the light of the Lord, illuminate all darkness in your life! May your faith in Jesus as the Son of God, make all the fear in you dissipate! May you see past the pain of your present circumstances, with the hope that looks forward to what the Lord has in-store for those who love Him! May the peace of the Lord, replace all the self talk that dominates you! May we all let God's word guide us, from chaos to clarity; replacing hate with love and pride with humility! In Jesus' mighty name, we pray!

November 5

May we stand for virtue and not fall for vice! May we embrace love and let go of hate! May we know the freedom from forgiveness, as we surrender resentments to Christ Jesus! May we not follow anger down that dead end road; but instead, be the peaceful restraint of patience! May we be a friend today, instead of a foe tomorrow! May we aspire to be every good thing in the world, through faith in Christ Jesus; then we will become that which we seek in the world and search no more! Moreover, love and peace will not elude us, but become our shadow, from the Lord's great light! In Jesus' loving name, may we meditate on all that is benevolent!

November 6

May I not look to the world with all it's possessions as fulfillment; but May I look to God's word, through faith in Christ Jesus, as the truth that frees my flesh from iniquity! The love of God, fulfills us beyond all understanding! Don't be mislead by the world and all the desires that leave people empty in the end! Know Jesus, and you shall know peace! Embrace the Grace of God, through faith in Christ Jesus and know the hope of Salvation! Seek the kingdom of God with all your heart, soul, mind and strength and you will find reconciliation with God the Father, through faith in His Son Jesus! May the love of the Lord, be the love you seek; so you search no more, and know the love that doesn't run out! Then go, and share that love with the world, to be called children of God! In Jesus' loving name!

November 7

This world is filled with trials and tribulations! God has given us a way out and a way through; with His precious Son Jesus, as our Savior! We who have faith in Christ, know the peace in chaos and the patience in overcoming difficulties! As we plow through addictions, impulsive and compulsive behaviors, obsessive thoughts in the mind and many other difficulties, we can find refuge, in Christ Jesus; by being in the yoke with Him! We are never alone; and can rejoice in all situations! For where we are weak, Christ Jesus is strong! May the love that brings everlasting peace from faith in Christ Jesus rest upon you always, In Jesus' mighty name!

November 8

As I surrender myself to the Lord, a transformation takes place in my character; I stop looking for what I can get out of life; and I start looking for what I can give to those who are in need! As my character grows through faith in Christ Jesus, my motives change completely! What matters to most, starts to dissipate. No longer do I strive for worldly things; but for things from above! My aspirations have become virtuous; not to bring glory to my name, but to bring Glory to God! In Jesus' mighty name, may the light of the lord, become our guide in everything we do!

November 9

To put on the body of Christ, is to be love in all it's forms! To be quick to serve, listen, forgive and be kind in a generous way! To be like Jesus, the Son of God, is to aspire to do great things in His name; Bringing Glory and honor to Him, who saved us all, from the wage of sin; through Faith! As we die to selfishness, in every way; we are born anew, in an altruistic (selfless) way; being the essence of humility, we put the least among us, before ourselves, with loving service! With great joy, we give back to God, by loving one another, without hidden motives for self! In Jesus' mighty name, let's be the love of God today, through faith in Christ Jesus!

November 10

Our God, is the Lord over this world and the one to come! We thank you God, for the opportunity to see the next world, through faith in your Son! Anyone who knows the Son, already knows the Father! For the Father and Son are one Light, one Truth and one Love! As we now know the light through Christ, we resist the darkness! As we stand for the truth of Christ Jesus, the lie in the world has no place in us anymore! As we love our neighbors as ourselves, we honor the love Christ Jesus bestowed on us, in His Holy Sacrifice! In Jesus' mighty name, let's all follow His light, so we don't lose our way in this sinful world!

November 11

Death could not hold Christ Jesus; because He is the truth of God! He is the Messiah; and anyone who puts their faith in Him, shall live and never die! Jesus is one with the breath of life; and nothing evil dwells in His glorious light of love! He is one with the FATHER of all creation! To love Christ Jesus, is to love the FATHER! To be loved by Christ Jesus, is to be loved by the FATHER! To know Christ Jesus, is to know the FATHER! May Jesus, in His Holy name, guide the lost to Him; as the Great Shepherd does for His lost sheep! In Jesus' mighty name, we pray!

November 12

When we speak love to one another, may our motives be altruistic (selfless)! May we speak with acts of kindness and use words to fulfill the heart, mind and spirit of another! The truth is, that we never had so much love, until we shared all of ours with another! No greater love than this, to lay down ones life for another (friends)! Thank you Christ Jesus, for the perfect example of love! In Jesus' loving name, may we emulate the love of Christ; by serving one another with no hidden motives!

November 13

It is Glory to God the Father, that we know the Son, Jesus the Christ! The word of life, is one with the Father; Christ Jesus is the word of God! As Jesus is one with the Father, we are called to be one with the Son; through faith, Jesus will intercede on our behalf!

The word is truth; and the one who denies that truth, is not with the Father! Embrace the truth of Christ Jesus and the Father will embrace you! All Glory to God the Father, who enlightens us all through faith in Christ Jesus and by the power of the Holy Spirit! In Jesus' mighty name, may the word of God (Yeshua/Jesus) be alive in us all! It is right to give all Praise and Glory to God our Father!

November 14

The word of God is truth and Christ Jesus is the word of God! May we stand with the truth and not fall for the persuasiveness of the lie! For the truth came to serve others and the lie serves only self! Don't delight in all forms of debauchery; which brings short lived satisfaction and everlasting death! Delight in the word of God, through faith in Christ Jesus; which brings everlasting peace! In Jesus' mighty name, may those lost in the lie, embrace the truth today, through faith in Christ Jesus!

November 15

Our joy for the day, comes from the positive projection of Christ Jesus in our future before we arrive!

Our hope is in the Lord and not in ourselves! We are optimistic in our faith in the Son of God!

We look past all difficulties, with great joy in our heart! We see trials as opportunities to grow in character and strengthen our Faith in Christ Jesus! May we all persevere with courage and strength that comes from Faith in God, through His Son Jesus! In Jesus' mighty name, we pray for all!

November 16

As children of God and saved by Faith in Christ Jesus; we have an obligation to spread the good news to all! We share the love of Christ, through good works for the poor; Being kind, to those who are not; Sharing what we have, with those that don't have anything! Speaking words of encouragement, to those who are discouraged! Our character speaks louder than words! We study the word of God, to share the truth! We stand for the truth of Christ Jesus, and we don't fall for the lie of the flesh! May the Holy Spirit of Truth, be yoked with us always, as we proclaim the good news of Christ Jesus to all; in His mighty name!

November 17

Our goal for the day is to share the good news of Christ Jesus, by being the love of God! We speak about Jesus in character, and emulate the Prince of Peace in every way! We share the Gospel with all; and go to great lengths for those who want to learn more! Our goal is to bring faithful servants to Christ Jesus; so they may be saved by the Grace of God! Our goal is not about accumulating materialistic stuff in the world for self! May we be the light of the Lord to all, in Jesus' Holy name!

November 18

We who know Christ Jesus as our Lord and Savior share Him with all those that doubt and are imprisoned from addictions, obsessive thoughts and sinful behavior! Jesus the Christ, is the key to freedom from all debauchery! He is the freedom from sinfulness; through faith and repentance! No one is without sin; and we all need Christ Jesus to intercede on our behalf! May we convey the message of the Gospel with love and not condemnation; to all those that suffer in their sinfulness! In Jesus' Holy name, we pray!

November 19

May our Lord and Savior, Jesus the Christ, be with us always; to help guide us, in serving others before ourselves! May we stay grateful for all that the Prince of Peace has sacrificed for our Salvation! May the magnitude of God's love through Christ Jesus, propel us forward to share the love of God with everyone! May our focus be of virtue, in guiding others from vice! May our motives be about bringing GLORY to God and not ourselves! In Jesus' mighty name, let's meditate on all the ways love can be expressed today!

November 20

In the Holy name of Jesus, I surrender all that is contrary to thy will! Guide me with your light; that is love in every way! May I be quick to forgive all insults; and walk away from all conflicts! May the wisdom of the Lord rest upon me, as I guide others in your mighty name! May I remain gentle around aggressiveness; and humble around the proud! May I delight in your truth dear Jesus; and emulate your love to all! In Jesus' mighty name, I pray!

November 21

As we come to you Father God, we come to the truth through your Son Jesus! We have all lost our way in this life! Now we choose to follow the word of life! Christ Jesus is the word! In the beginning was the word and the word was with God; and the word was God! We make a beginning through faith in your word, and our Savior, Christ Jesus your Son! We stand for your truth, and we stop falling for the lie in this world! In Jesus' mighty name, may your love be expressed by us, through the word of life alive in our hearts!

November 22

When you want to act out to injustice and hurt the people hurting you, remember how God handled the crucifixion, of His loving Son Jesus! We are to emulate that same love and patience, that God showed us! We trust God in all situations; and His love and judgements are sufficient in all trials, tribulations and tragedies! Faith is more than belief; it's trusting that which we cannot see! God, I trust you with every situation in my life! Furthermore, I trust you with my life and the lives that are precious to me! In Jesus' mighty name, I pray that we all have the Faith that trusts God in every situation!

November 23

When Jesus the Christ walked among us as a man, He gave us many lessons on how we should walk and talk; how we should pray and have faith; and how we should love and serve the least among us, with authentic humility! May we internalize His words of truth! Analyze and surrender everything in us that blocks that truth! Furthermore, we should utilize His ways to serve one another, with the same love He served us with! This is the new creation, through faith in Christ Jesus, that brings salvation into fruition! Lord, we honor your great gift, with the love we convey for one another; in Jesus' Holy name!

November 24

My life is yours God! For you gave this life to me; therefore, it's only right that I live to serve you!

"THANKSGIVING"

May I bring the love of your Son Jesus, to all I greet!
May I give the hungry, food to eat!
May I smile, to the face with a frown!
May I pick up those, who happen to fall down!
May I live to give and show love to all!
May I teach Grace, to all who fall!

May the gratitude in our hearts, for all that God has done for us through Christ Jesus; propel us forward with thanksgiving, to help all those in need!

November 25

Lord Jesus, we thank you for your Holy sacrifice, for the sins of the world! As you died for the forgiveness of sins, we also must forgive, if we want to be forgiven! There is freedom in forgiveness!

Freedom to love, instead of the prison to hate! Freedom to form friendships, instead of creating many foes! Holding no record of wrongs is giving the Grace we embrace, through faith in Christ Jesus! In Jesus' mighty name, may we forgive everything done to us and to the ones we love!

November 26

Every time we express love in one form or another, we embrace God through that expression! God is love; and therefore, the love given with no hidden motives becomes one with God! Jesus was the gift of love from God! Jesus taught us the value of love above all else in this world! When we put love first, for God, through His altruistic Son, we are perfected through Faith in the Son and His love for us! We are to extend that same love to one another, regardless of the other persons behavior! We may not like what people do, but we are now son's and daughters of the most High God, through Christ Jesus; and we are the branches of love, from the one true Vine! In Jesus' mighty name, may we put the love of God, above all else today!

November 27

As we do our best to move away from sin (repent), we follow the word of God (Christ Jesus)! The word is light and no darkness can be found in that light! Our old selves are dead; and we don't live in the guilt, shame and remorse of our past! We live in Christ Jesus and He lives in us through faith! In that faith, there is no record of wrongs; because Christ Jesus did not die in vain! We are saved by faith and we are guided by the light of Christ; not by the darkness of our past! In the Grace of God, there is freedom from our sins, opinions of others and all forms of guilt! Embrace the Grace of God, through faith in Christ Jesus! In Jesus' mighty name, may we all share the good news (Gospel) about the Grace of God, through faith in Christ Jesus!

November 28

As servants of the Lord, we look to serve and not be served, with the love of Christ Jesus! We boast only about what Jesus has done for us! If any pride be in us, may it be in serving the least among us, in Jesus' loving name! May everything we do, bring Glory to God's name and not our own! May others be attracted to the kindness we express, so they want to know more about our faith in Christ Jesus! The attraction is in our character and the promotion is in the love we express to everyone! Let's be the light of the Lord, in someone's darkness today, in Jesus' mighty name!

November 29

Jesus the Christ is our Savior! He took every evil thing in this world upon Himself, although no evil was in Him! He knows our struggles and the struggles we caused others! Let's all move away from such sinfulness! The benevolence of Jesus is alive in us all; through faith in Him, as the Son of God! We follow Him through His word, which is alive in His faithful children! The Great Shepherd, Guides His sheep from harm! Heaven rejoices, as we are saved from eternal damnation! We thank you Father, for you extending yourself, through your Son Yeshua (Jesus)! In Jesus' mighty name, let's share the good news of Christ Jesus, to all believers and non-believers alike!

November 30

As we all come to the Father, through faith in Christ Jesus; we bring others with us, through the extension of love! For as God is love, we are called to be love! Christ Jesus, taught us how to be the expression of love to all! For when we do anything for the least among us, we do for the Father and the Son; who are one! In Jesus' mighty name, may we be the love we seek through faith in Christ Jesus, so we search no more; and share that love world wide!

December 1

The Lord guides us with His word, and the wise follow it with joy! The fool tries to punch holes in the truth, to avoid guilt from their lies! Christ Jesus is truth; and His word restores all that is broken in us! There is life in the Lord, for all that believe in Him! Do not entertain what the lost believe; but reject every form of sin! Do not sway with the wind of sin in this world; but look with hope, for the sunlight of the spirit, in the world to come! In Jesus' mighty name, let's live by examples of virtues and not by vice (immoral or wicked behavior!)

December 2

May the peaceful restraint of the Lord be upon me, as my enemies plot against me! May the mercy afforded me through faith in Christ Jesus, help me to be more compassionate! May I be content in who God created me to be; and use that to help others! May I put others before myself, as Christ did for all of us! May I remain humble when I succeed and share the proceeds, with those in need! The love of the Lord, is an action word, that brings much kindness into every situation! In Jesus' loving name, may we express loving kindness to the lost and less fortunate!

December 3

My love for you Lord, does not run out! It is expressed with acts of kindness in your name! You are the joy in my smile and the hope in my thoughts! All that is good in me, is you! Jesus the Christ is love; and my love is one with He! There is nothing selfish in that love! It is authentically altruistic! Only by dying to all forms of selfishness, can I stay connected to this awesome love! There is liberation and strength in this love! No sin can be found in this love! You take all my sins away, through faith in thee! As I become this love through you, I search no more; Now love does not elude me, but has become my shadow, from your great light!

December 4

To have faith in Christ Jesus, is to remain in the light of hope, when difficult times come into our life! Through faith in the Son of God, we can persevere through anything life gives us! Our strength comes from knowing the truth about the Messiah; and that truth sets us free in this life and the next! May we look to serve others with this hope in the Lord, so they may see past their present circumstances! In Christ Jesus' mighty name, we pray!

December 5

Lord, I am a lost man without you! It's through faith in you Jesus, that I am filled with the Holy Spirit; which brings the good news of the Gospel to all! It's by Faith, that all things come into fruition! Of myself, I fall short of the glory of God! I strive for righteousness and fall short everyday; but my Faith in you, saves me from the law, that I can not fulfill! I am so grateful to you God; that I propel forward with enthusiasm about the good news of Salvation, through Faith in your Son Jesus the Christ! I share this as a feast, among starving people for the truth! Some refuse to eat the word of God and starve! Others can't get enough and want to share what's been given! There's plenty that comes from you oh God! May we invite all to dine with us on the body of Christ Jesus, so the word of God can be alive in us; and expressed through the loving service, we provide for the poor in spirit! In Jesus' mighty name, I pray!

December 6

By the power of the Holy Spirit and through faith in Christ Jesus, may we all greet hate with the Lords love! May we express gentleness, instead of being aggressive towards all negativity! We no longer conduct ourselves the way we used to; furthermore, may we stay above reproach, no matter what the circumstances are! For we are children of the most high God, through faith in Christ Jesus! May we act as such, in Jesus' loving name!

December 7

May our faith in Christ Jesus give us the discernment (understanding) of Gods will; by the power of the Holy Spirit! May we all be obedient (live by virtue) to the word of God, that Christ Jesus spoke to us all! As we move away from sin (repent), we put others before ourselves (humility)! In Jesus' mighty name, may we all be yoked to Jesus; and may His strength be perfected in our weakness!

December 8

In the Grace of God, through faith in Christ Jesus, there is no record of wrongs! Peace and love dwell in the Grace of God! As we give the grace we embrace, we come to a new place in our lives! The more we give away, the more peace and love we feel from within! God is in us all; and we connect with God when we are in compliance with His will! In Jesus' mighty name, may we all emulate the peace and love of our Lord and Savior Yeshua Hamashiach (Jesus the Messiah!)

December 9

We pray in Jesus' Holy name, that we emulate Christ Jesus' loving humility; by the power of the Holy Spirit of Truth! May we set aside our desires of the flesh; and stand for the spirit! May we who are faithful to the Lord, speak through our character, more than our words! We put the struggles that other people are experiencing, before ourselves, in true humility! In Jesus' mighty name, may we all be examples of Christ Jesus' loving humility!

December 10

The destructive patterns of our lives, have been replaced by gentle cycles of love; being conveyed in what we say and do! As we emulate the truth of Christ Jesus, we become one with love in all its forms! May our focus be in the transformation from self-centeredness, to a God consciousness! Furthermore, let's not be dominated by our past mistakes, but motivated to serve all, through the Grace of God; and by the power of the Holy Spirit!

December 11

When I look to you with faith God, you're always there to guide me! Your love is never ending and your wisdom no one can understand! Help me to be obedient in all my ways; and to serve the least among us! May I never question you in anyway; but trust you with all things through Christ Jesus, your Son! Where your light is, no darkness can be found! May I meditate on your love all day long and share it with everyone! For your love is expressed through Christ Jesus, our Lord and Savior! That love is the truth that sets us all free! In Jesus' mighty name, help me to be the love that brings clarity into someone's confusion; and the light of compassion into someone who is suffering in darkness!

December 12

The Lord speaks through His children in character! The word of life, that was with God in the beginning; is with all those who believe that Christ Jesus is the Son of God! We all fall short of the glory of God; yet, Jesus the Christ intercedes on our behalf! We are set right through faith in the Messiah and not by our own accord, so no one can boast! May Jesus, who is the word of God; speak through all those willing to carry His message of hope and promise of freedom from the wage of sin!

December 13

COMPLETE SURRENDER PRAYER

God, take my pride and my ego and turn it into humility and keep me humble; take my lust and turn it into purity and keep me faithful in my marriage; take my hate, anger and resentment and turn it into love, acceptance and forgiveness; Take my laziness and turn it into ambition and motivation; take my greed and turn it into generosity and sharing; take my gluttony and turn it into moderation and balance; take my envy and my jealousy and turn it into contentment; help me to be more like you dear Jesus and less like myself!

December 14

As we navigate through many trials, tribulations and tragedies in this life, our faith in Christ Jesus sustains us all! We no longer walk through difficulties aimlessly and alone; but by faith in Christ Jesus. The Holy Spirit of Truth, guides us towards the Light of God! In that light, is peace beyond all understanding! In Jesus' mighty name, we pray that the Holy Spirit of Truth, gives us the words to guide the lost to God!

December 15

To hear the word of God, is to have the seed of Grace in ones mind! To understand the Holy Sacrifice of Christ Jesus, is to plant that seed in fertile soil! To meditate on the word of God, is to become the love we seek in all our relationships; and give sunlight to that seed! To share the word of God, is to feed the world from the harvest of that seed; that grew to a ripe fruit! To eat the word of God, is to internalize the truth of Christ Jesus and become one with the Holy Spirit! In Jesus' mighty name!

December 16

The inspiration of Gods word, is my motivation and guides my aspirations! I shall not bargain or negotiate with any form of sin! The truth of Christ Jesus, sets us all free from the destructiveness of sin! God builds us up in His ways, for those with a steadfast faith in Christ Jesus! As we plow through the temptations of sin, yoked to Christ Jesus, we become vessels of light to all those caught in their sinful darkness! In Jesus' mighty name, may we who know Christ Jesus, guide others by the power of the Holy Spirit; and not by our sinful nature!

December 17

The generosity of the Lord is inspired by a loving faith, and not by works! The light of the Lord comforts those lost in darkness! He is the refuge for the abused! The peace of the Lord dissipates all chaos! For those who seek Christ Jesus, they will be comforted! All that have faith in the Son of God will be saved from the wage of sin! How great thou art, no one knows; yet you value all with the same love! I am humbled by your majestic power! May I serve thee all the days of my life, by expressing your word to all who will receive it! In Jesus' mighty name, I pray!

December 18

For all that live by the law and not by faith in Christ Jesus, are missing out on God's promise of Salvation! No one is justified with God on their own accord! We all need Christ Jesus to intercede on our behalf; and we all need to be saved! Surrender your thinking of another way! There is no other way! Christ Jesus is the way, and the only way! If there was another way, He who is truth, would have told us! In Jesus' mighty name, may we all stand together in Faith; and not fall for the erroneous options of the world!

December 19

As God is love; we are called to be that love, through faith in Christ Jesus! As we meditate on love, we meditate on all that is good in love! We look to serve and not be served! To listen and not be heard! We look to lay down our lives so others may benefit! Our motives are benevolent, through Gods love in us! In Jesus' loving name, help us all to express Gods love, to the doubter and the faithful alike!

December 20

May I be quick to listen to the Lord; and may His Commandments be etched into my heart! May I carry love from place to place, with acts of kindness in His mighty name! May my faith in Christ Jesus not falter, in times of distress! Now that I know Grace through Faith, may I hold no grudges towards anyone! May the light of the Lord rest upon me, to serve others and not myself! In Jesus' Holy name, may these words patch the emptiness in those that are suffering!

December 21

For those of us that choose to take Christ Jesus into our hearts; we know a new peace from that faith! The peace is not an illusion, but a fact that the Holy Spirit of truth has become a part of us! The transformation from insanity, to tranquility is evident to us and others! Where there is the love of the Lord, peace becomes it's shadow; from the Lords Great Light! We no longer entertain the darkness of this world, because we look to be with God in the next! Our positive projection through faith in Christ Jesus helps us to persevere through anything! In Jesus' mighty name, may all doubters internalize the truth of Christ Jesus and stop denying the Son of God!

December 22

We are called to do much through our faith in Christ Jesus; but it is little compared to the Glory of God, which we will receive through faith in His only begotten Son! As disciples of Christ Jesus, we emulate the love that serves all, in our Father's name! We trust Gods word, through His entrusted Apostles, of Christ Jesus! We share the body of Christ, with all who want to internalize the truth of God, by the power of the Holy Spirit; in Jesus' mighty name!

December 23

Jesus the Christ is truth; and that truth is one with God; and is God! Those who reject this truth have not looked at the proof in the prophecies fulfilled by Christ Jesus, in the book of life (Bible)! Blessed are those that believe without seeing! Blessed are those who repent of their sins and take Christ Jesus into their hearts as their Lord and Savior! For all those that stay in doubt about Christ Jesus, I pray they see the truth through the word of God; and stand for the faith that prevails over everything, in Jesus' mighty name!

December 24

May the chaos of this world and the doubters of the most high God, have no interference with our faith in Christ Jesus; but propel us who have faith, to embrace the love of God completely! As we become the love of God, through faith in Christ Jesus, we search no more; then love does not elude us, but becomes our shadow, from the Lords great light! We become disciples of love, through faith in Christ Jesus, by spreading the good news (Gospel) of having faith in the Lord! We live in the clarity of Gods love through faith in His Son, Jesus, the Christ! Therefore, the clarity of Gods love, overcomes all the chaos of the world's hate, in Jesus' loving name!

December 25

JESUS

From the kingdom of light, you left your throne; born at night, all alone! The virgin gave birth, to the king of kings! The star shined over the earth, as the angels did sing! Salvation became possible, on that day; in the name of Jesus, people would say! Your walk in life, became so great; You removed the strife and increased the faith! You fulfilled all that was written, from many before; and nothing was missing, as heaven opened its door! Death couldn't defeat you, and Satan wouldn't win; it's through faith in Christ Jesus, that Salvation can begin!

Remember, every day we celebrate Christ Jesus coming into the world!

December 26

When I stand for the truth of Christ Jesus, every weakness in my character is exposed! Every lie has to be surrendered; so His truth can come into fruition in my life! As I surrender the illusion of myself, I'm introduced to my authentic self! This new being looks to serve the least among Himself, in true humility! There's liberty in exposing the lie and standing for the truth of God, through faith in His Son Jesus! I look with new eyes and hear with new ears! My perception of reality is not blocked, by my false ego! Therefore, I build authentic relationships for the first time and they grow exponentially! In Jesus' loving name!

December 27

The power of the Holy Spirit is truth; received from our faith in Christ Jesus! The Mercy of our Lord is everlasting and illuminates our souls! His light is love, and guides us all in this life and the next! Our Hope is in the Lord alone! With thanksgiving in our hearts, we share with all, the good news of Christ Jesus! As we freely received through faith; we freely give in love and fellowship! In Jesus' mighty name, let's all emulate the kindness of our Lord and Savior!

December 28

We are to conform to Christ Jesus and His generous love that is expressed with deep compassion for the lost and suffering! Living by every virtue and dying to all selfishness! If we wouldn't do it in front of God, then don't do it! Don't bargain or negotiate with any form of sin, or it will have its way with you; leading to death for a short time of pleasure and long suffering to follow! Don't be tormented by living contrary to the will of God! Hold fast to the commandments of our Lord and Savior Christ Jesus, and you will become the love and peace you seek in the world! For the world will fail you, but in Christ Jesus, you will be fulfilled!

December 29

When you see the light through Christ Jesus, enter it, and don't look back to your lost ways in darkness! Come to the Lord, one and all! For in the light, is love; that brings peace into every situation! The Lord of light, drives out all darkness! Surrender yourselves to the Lord, and you will not lack in anything! All that you desire in the flesh, is fleeting; but in the Spirit of God, through Faith in Christ Jesus, you will know fulfillment! May the light of the Lord, rest upon the faithful forever, in Jesus' mighty name!

December 30

As I put on the love of Christ Jesus, evil can't have its way with me; for the love of our Lord is light; and no darkness from this world or the next can extinguish it! As I spread the good news of our Lord and Savior, my character becomes a compassionate love to all! I am responsible for planting the seed of love through faith in the Son of God; and I leave the rest to God! For in faith is trust and I don't debate about the truth of Christ Jesus! He is and I am through Him; the love I always searched for! Yet what kind of love would I be if I didn't share it with everyone? The love from me comes from Christ and is given, not earned! I may not like what you do, but God's love is more powerful than any sinner! We must be the light of love in all darkness, through Christ Jesus; for He is the light of this world and the next! In Jesus' mighty name, let's be the love of Christ Jesus and search no more! Then love will not elude us, but become our shadow, from His magnificent light!

December 31

As we turn away from our old self through faith in Christ Jesus, we are born again as a new creation of hope! We abide in this new hope, through the word of God, who is Christ Jesus! We resist sin and stay sanctified through faith in the Messiah! Christ Jesus is He! By embracing this truth, we are set forth on the right path of love, in all its forms! We become the love of Christ to all by faith! No one has to earn our love, because we emulate the Mercy of God, through His Son Jesus! We give, because it was given to us first! In Jesus' loving name, may we love one another, as Christ Jesus has loved us!

God Turned Me Around

Many will hate me now; but I won't stop now!
I'm turning that frown, upside down!
I was that lost one, in the town; but Christ Jesus, is what I found!
So I won't stop now; for love I found!
I'm gonna be kind, in the Town!
I'm sorry God; I let so many down!
I'm gonna turn it around!
Look close; a new me God found!
I once was down; but Christ Jesus turned it around!
It's Grace I found! When I let everyone down! God saved me now!
Let me show you how!
It's through faith and not doubt! that is how; let's not stop now!
Let's show others how!
We can turn hate into love; in any Town!
Start with a smile, and resist that frown!
Let's turn all the hate, upside down; and be the love; in every city and Town!
God help me now; for Christ Jesus showed us how!
I love you all; so please don't doubt me now!
If God saved me; He can turn anyone around!
So don't stop now; for love is how!
We can turn it around! Jesus the Christ is how!

MIKE PETROSINO